berries

berries

SWEET & SAVORY RECIPES

eliza cross

Photographs by Stacey Cramp

GIBBS SMITH
TO ENRICH AND INSPIRE HUMANKIND

For Amy Ostwald Villwock

First Edition
21 20 19 18 17   5 4 3 2 1

Text © 2017 Eliza Cross
Photographs © 2017 Stacey Cramp

Published by
Gibbs Smith
P.O. Box 667
Layton, Utah 84041

1.800.835.4993 orders
www.gibbs-smith.com

Designed by Katie Jennings Campbell
Food styling by Vanessa Seder
Printed and bound in Hong Kong

Gibbs Smith books are printed on paper produced from sustainable PEFC-certified forest/controlled wood source. Learn more at www.pefc.org.

Library of Congress Cataloging-in-Publication Data

Names: Cross, Eliza, author. | Cramp, Stacey, photographer.
Title: Berries : sweet and savory recipes / Eliza Cross ; photographs by Stacey Cramp.
Description: First edition. | Layton, Utah : Gibbs Smith, [2016] | Includes index.
Identifiers: LCCN 2016031410 | ISBN 9781423644590 (hardcover)
Subjects: LCSH: Cooking (Berries) | LCGFT: Cookbooks.
Classification: LCC TX813.B4 C76 2016 | DDC 641.6/47--dc23
LC record available at https://lccn.loc.gov/2016031410

Contents

Introduction

Fresh berries are among nature's most delightful treats, and nearly everyone seems to have a sweet, vivid memory involving berries. Perhaps you recall gratefully eating handfuls of wild blackberries discovered during a long hike, or raiding the sun-ripened raspberries straight from the thorny canes in your mother's summer garden, or picking tiny ruby-red wild currants in a mountain meadow to make homemade jelly.

Berries still grow wild in some parts of the country, so it is still quite possible to experience the pleasurable surprise of discovering a stand of overgrown blueberry bushes or tasting a tiny sun-ripened alpine strawberry. Modern farming and shipping methods mean that we can buy many types of fresh and frozen berries year round at the market.

If finding berries is easy, defining and cataloging the diminutive fruits is a bit more complicated. Strawberries and raspberries do not fit the botanical definition of a fleshy fruit derived from a single ovary, so they are considered aggregate fruits rather than berries. On the other hand, avocados are technically considered berries, as are tomatoes, grapes, watermelons, eggplants—and even bananas. Who knew?

For the recipes in this book, we sidestepped the botanical definitions and used the most widely available fruits that we commonly think of as berries: blueberries, raspberries, blackberries, boysenberries, strawberries, and cranberries. Feel free to experiment and substitute your own favorite regional and native berries. Huckleberries, bilberries, and juneberries can often replace blueberries, for example, while marionberries, loganberries, boysenberries, mulberries, and raspberries will usually double for blackberries.

Berries are twice blessed since they offer amazing health benefits in addition to being downright delicious. Deeply colored berries like blueberries and blackberries contain some of the highest antioxidant levels of foods measured by the USDA. Antioxidants protect the body from damage caused by free radicals, and may even help manage or prevent several medical conditions including dementia and some cancers. When they are available, we prefer organic, wild, or homegrown berries to avoid the pesticide residue that can sometimes remain on conventionally grown berries.

While berries have a well-deserved reputation for sweetening pies and desserts, they can add color and flavor to salads, main courses, sauces, salsas, smoothies, and more. We hope you enjoy this collection of recipes celebrating the sweet, tangy, irresistible flavor of nature's most delightful fruit.

Berry Picking & Prepping

SELECTION

When picking fresh berries in the wild or the garden, choose plump, deeply colored berries that slip easily from the stem; they are not fully ripe if you have to tug at them. Berries do not continue to ripen after being picked, so choose the ripest berries you can find. Roadside stands and farmers' markets are often good places to find fresh, ripe berries. When buying berries in plastic containers, inspect the bottom side for excess liquid or mold—two signs that you should choose another container. Finally, inspect the berries after you bring them home from the market, and discard any mushy, overripe, or moldy fruits right away.

CLEANING

If you discover bugs on freshly picked berries, make a salt water mixture with 1 cup of sea salt dissolved in 1 gallon of cool water. Soak the berries for 1 hour and rinse with cool water before using. Wait to gently rinse berries with cool water until just before eating or cooking with them. If you refrigerate delicate berries like raspberries and boysenberries for an hour before rinsing, they will be firmer and better able to sustain the rinsing process without damage.

Fresh strawberries have a leafy top called a hull, which will need to be removed (except for berries used for garnish). Pull off the leaves and use a small, sharp knife to cut a small cone from the top of the berry, or push a plastic drinking straw up from the bottom to the top of the berry to remove the hull. You can also use a small metal huller to pinch and twist off the hulls.

STORAGE

Store unwashed berries in the refrigerator, inside a paper towel-lined container to absorb moisture. Berries have a short shelf life and should be used in a day or two.

To freeze berries, rinse and dry them thoroughly. Spread them in a single layer on a parchment paper-lined pan or baking sheet, and freeze until solid. Then transfer to a ziplock freezer bag or airtight container. Use frozen berries within 6 months for best flavor. To thaw frozen berries, spread them in a shallow container, like a baking dish, cover, and refrigerate for 8 hours or overnight. Drain any accumulated juices.

SERVING

Room temperature berries have more flavor than chilled berries, so let raw berries sit out for 1 hour before serving. Very tart berries can be lightly sweetened with a drizzle of simple syrup. (To make simple syrup, combine 2 parts sugar and 1 part water in a saucepan; bring to a simmer over medium heat and cook, stirring, until sugar dissolves. Refrigerate in a covered container for up to 1 month.) Sliced strawberries can be macerated with sugar, which draws out the berries' natural juices and forms a sweet syrup for a tasty topping to spoon over a bowl of ice cream or a slice of cake. Hull and slice the berries, transfer to a bowl, sprinkle with granulated sugar, and let stand at room temperature, stirring occasionally, for 1 hour.

Beverages
&
Sweets

Strawberry-Mint Lemonade

Sweet strawberries are the perfect complement to tangy fresh-squeezed lemonade, making a summery drink that is as pretty as it is refreshing. This recipe can easily be doubled or tripled and served like punch for a bridal shower, luncheon, or party.

SERVES 12

8 cups water, divided

2 cups granulated sugar

1 pint fresh strawberries, hulled

12 fresh mint leaves, finely chopped

2 cups freshly squeezed lemon juice (about 8 lemons)

Mint sprigs, for garnish

Combine 2 cups of the water, the sugar, and the strawberries in a blender or food processor; process until mixture is smooth. Transfer to a pitcher and add the remaining 6 cups water, the mint leaves, and lemon juice. Stir until well combined.

Serve in tall glasses over ice, garnished with mint sprigs.

Purple Power Smoothie

Brain-boosting berries, potassium-rich bananas, and protein-filled Greek yogurt are blended for a satisfying drink that tastes more like a milkshake than a healthy smoothie.

SERVES 2

1/2 cup fresh or frozen (thawed and drained) blackberries or boysenberries

1/2 cup fresh or frozen (thawed and drained) blueberries

2/3 cup vanilla Greek yogurt

1 cup milk

1 banana, sliced

1 tablespoon honey

1/2 teaspoon vanilla extract

Combine all the ingredients in a blender or food processor. Pulse for 30 seconds, scrape down sides, and pulse for an additional 30 seconds.

Pour into 2 glasses and serve immediately.

Raspberry-Lime Sparklers

Evoking the flavors of a fruity mojito, this elegant nonalcoholic cocktail balances tart cranberries and lime juice with sweet fresh raspberries. The drink is topped with a splash of bubbly club soda and fragrant fresh mint. For an alcoholic sparkler, add a splash of light rum or vodka to each glass.

SERVES 6

1/4 cup granulated sugar

1/4 cup water

1/2 cup fresh or frozen (thawed and drained) raspberries

2 cups cranberry-raspberry juice

1/2 cup freshly squeezed lime juice (about 6 limes)

12 fresh mint leaves, roughly chopped

2 cups club soda

Mint sprigs, for garnish

Fresh lime slices, for garnish

In a small saucepan, combine the sugar and water. Heat over medium heat, stirring frequently, until sugar is completely dissolved. Remove from stove and cool to room temperature.

Pour the syrup in a pitcher and add the raspberries, cranberry-raspberry juice, lime juice, and mint leaves. Stir until combined, breaking up the raspberries and crushing the mint leaves with a spoon.

Add the club soda and stir gently. Serve in tall glasses over ice, garnished with mint sprigs and lime slices.

Cranberry Mulled Cider

Apple cider, cranberries, and citrus are enlivened with fresh ginger in this updated version of classic mulled cider. A side benefit? Your home will be filled with the irresistible aroma of cinnamon and cloves.

SERVES 8 TO 10

1 quart apple cider

2 cups cranberry juice

1 cup orange juice

1/2 cup freshly squeezed lemon juice (about 2 lemons)

1/2 cup granulated sugar

1 cup fresh or frozen (thawed and drained) whole cranberries

2 whole cinnamon sticks

1 (1-inch) fresh ginger root, peeled

3 whole cloves

Combine the cider, cranberry juice, orange juice, lemon juice, and sugar in a large saucepan over medium heat. Stir until sugar dissolves and add the cranberries, cinnamon sticks, ginger, and cloves. Bring the mixture to a light simmer, reduce heat, and continue simmering mixture, covered, for 15 minutes. Discard the cinnamon sticks, ginger, and cloves. Pour cider into warmed mugs and serve.

Perfect Strawberry Milk Shakes

Fresh strawberries add vibrant flavor to this old-fashioned soda fountain favorite. A dash of malted milk powder adds an authentic touch.

SERVES 4

1/2 pound fresh strawberries, sliced

2 tablespoons granulated sugar

1 teaspoon vanilla extract

1 pint strawberry ice cream

1 cup whole milk, plus more if needed

1 tablespoon malted milk powder

Red sparkling sugar, for garnish

4 fresh strawberries, for garnish

Chill four 12-ounce glasses in the refrigerator.

Meanwhile, place the sliced strawberries in a freezerproof bowl. Sprinkle with the sugar and vanilla then stir to coat the berries. Cover and chill in the freezer for 1 hour. During the last 15 minutes of chilling, remove the ice cream from the freezer to soften at room temperature.

Remove the berry mixture from the freezer and transfer to a blender or food processor. Add 3/4 cup of the milk and the malted milk powder then blend until mixture is smooth. Spoon in the ice cream and pour in the remaining 1/4 cup milk. Blend until smooth, adding more milk if needed. Pour the mixture into the chilled glasses and sprinkle with the red sparkling sugar. Garnish each milk shake with a strawberry.

Patriotic Stuffed Strawberries

These bite-sized treats are perfect for Independence Day or any time you want to celebrate the red, white, and blue.

MAKES ABOUT 24 STRAWBERRIES

1½ pounds large fresh strawberries

8 ounces cream cheese, softened

½ cup powdered sugar

¼ teaspoon almond extract

½ cup fresh blueberries

Cut a thin slice from the top of each strawberry. Turn the strawberries over on a cutting board, trimming the berries if necessary so they sit flat. Using a sharp knife, cut an X inside each berry from the tip to about ¼ inch from the bottom. (Do not cut all the way through.) Reserve.

In a medium bowl, combine the cream cheese, powdered sugar, and almond extract; beat with an electric mixer until light and fluffy, 1 to 2 minutes. Transfer the mixture to a pastry bag fitted with a large star tip.

Gently open each strawberry and pipe the filling inside. Top each filled strawberry with a blueberry. Arrange the strawberries on a serving platter and refrigerate for 1 hour before serving.

Raspberry Truffles

Simple and elegant, these rich chocolate truffles are each topped with a perfect ruby-red raspberry. They are guaranteed to be a hit at a party or potluck.

MAKES 24 TRUFFLES

12 ounces best-quality semisweet chocolate

3/4 cup heavy cream

3 tablespoons raspberry liqueur (such as framboise) or raspberry syrup

24 blemish-free fresh raspberries

Chop the chocolate very finely and transfer it to a medium heatproof bowl.

Heat the cream in a small saucepan over medium heat just until it starts to simmer. Immediately pour the hot cream over the chocolate and allow to rest for 1 minute. Stir until smooth. Add the liqueur and stir until smooth.

Line a 24-cup mini muffin pan with paper candy cups. Spoon 1 rounded tablespoon of warm ganache into each cup and press 1 raspberry into the center. Repeat with remaining cups. Cover lightly with plastic wrap and refrigerate until firm, about 2 hours.

Blueberry Cheesecake Fudge

Enjoy the tantalizing flavors of creamy blueberry-topped cheesecake in one bite with this easy recipe. Arranged in a pretty tin, homemade fudge makes a welcome gift for holidays and other occasions. For a classic winter taste, substitute cranberries for the blueberries.

MAKES 81 SQUARES

1/4 cup unsalted butter

2 1/2 cups granulated sugar

2/3 cup evaporated milk

3 cups miniature marshmallows

6 ounces cream cheese, softened

1 (12-ounce) bag white chocolate chips

8 ounces dried blueberries

2 teaspoons vanilla extract

Line a 9 x 9-inch square pan with aluminum foil, extending the foil by 1 inch on two opposite sides, and spray lightly with nonstick cooking spray.

In a large saucepan over medium heat, combine the butter, sugar, milk, and marshmallows. Bring to a rolling boil, stirring constantly, until a candy thermometer reaches 234 degrees F, about 5 minutes. Remove from heat and stir in the cream cheese and chocolate chips until smooth and melted. Add the blueberries and vanilla and stir until blended.

Pour the fudge into the prepared pan, smooth the top, and cool to room temperature. Lift from pan using foil. Peel off foil and cut fudge into 1-inch squares. Store in an airtight container in the refrigerator for up to 1 week.

Jams,
Preserves
&
Sauces

Blueberry-Lemon Jam

The bright, vibrant flavors of blueberries burst forth in this easy jam recipe. A touch of lemon and honey adds complexity and balance.

MAKES 7 (8-OUNCE) JARS

4½ cups fresh or frozen (thawed and drained) blueberries

4½ cups granulated sugar

1¾ cups honey

⅓ cup freshly squeezed lemon juice (1 to 2 lemons)

2 teaspoons grated lemon rind

5 tablespoons classic powdered pectin

Prepare a water bath canner. Sterilize 7 half-pint jars, lids, and rings; keep them hot.

Combine the blueberries, sugar, honey, lemon juice, and lemon rind in a 6-quart Dutch oven or heavy-bottomed pot over high heat. Bring to a rolling boil, stirring frequently. Add the pectin and stir to combine. Boil for 1 minute, stirring constantly. Remove from heat and skim off any foam, if necessary.

Immediately ladle the jam into hot jars, leaving ¼-inch headspace. Wipe the rims of the jars with a damp paper towel. Tap the jars to remove any air bubbles, screw on the caps, and process them in the water bath canner for 15 minutes, or the time recommended for your area by your county extension agent. Cool the jars and press the top of each lid with a finger, ensuring the seal is tight and that the lid does not move up or down at all. (If any jars have not sealed properly, refrigerate them and eat the jam within 2 weeks.) Store sealed jars in a cool, dark place.

Summer Essence Raspberry Jam

No pectin is needed in this deeply flavored, ruby-red raspberry jam. With just three ingredients, it is also quick and easy to prepare.

MAKES 4 (8-OUNCE) JARS

---

4 cups granulated sugar

4 cups fresh raspberries

1/4 cup freshly squeezed lemon juice (about 1 lemon)

Preheat the oven to 250 degrees F. Prepare a water bath canner. Sterilize 4 half-pint jars, lids, and rings; keep them hot.

Spread the sugar in a shallow baking pan. Bake for 15 minutes.

Meanwhile, pour the berries and lemon juice in a large heavy-bottomed saucepan and mash with a potato masher. Turn the heat to high and bring to a full boil, stirring constantly. Remove the sugar from the oven and add to the berries. Return the mixture to a boil, stirring constantly, until the temperature measures 220 degrees F on an instant-read thermometer, 5 to 8 minutes.

Remove jam from heat and skim off any foam, if necessary. Immediately ladle into hot jars, leaving 1/4-inch headspace. Wipe the rims of the jars with a damp paper towel. Tap the jars to remove any air bubbles, screw on the caps, and process them in the water bath canner for 15 minutes, or the time recommended for your area by your county extension agent. Cool the jars and press the top of each lid with a finger, ensuring the seal is tight and that the lid does not move up or down at all. (If any jars have not sealed properly, refrigerate them and eat the jam within 2 weeks.) Store sealed jars in a cool, dark place.

Jumbleberry Jam

This fun-to-pronounce jam is perfect for people who have a hard time choosing just one favorite berry flavor. Feel free to experiment and mix the berries in any proportion you like.

MAKES 6 (8-OUNCE) JARS

4 cups crushed mixed fresh or frozen (thawed and drained) berries of your choice

$4\frac{1}{2}$ tablespoons classic powdered pectin

3 cups sugar

Prepare a water bath canner. Sterilize 6 half-pint jars, lids, and rings; keep them hot.

Combine the berries and pectin in a 6-quart Dutch oven or heavy-bottomed pot over high heat. Bring to a rolling boil, stirring frequently. Add the sugar and stir until dissolved. Return mixture to a full rolling boil. Boil for 1 minute, stirring constantly. Remove jam from heat and skim off any foam, if necessary.

Immediately ladle jam into hot jars, leaving $\frac{1}{4}$-inch headspace. Wipe the rims of the jars with a damp paper towel. Tap the jars to remove any air bubbles, screw on the caps, and process them in the water bath canner for 15 minutes, or the time recommended for your area by your county extension agent. Cool the jars and press the top of each lid with a finger, ensuring the seal is tight and that the lid does not move up or down at all. (If any jars have not sealed properly, refrigerate them and eat the jam within 2 weeks.) Store sealed jars in a cool, dark place.

Seedless Blackberry Jam

Whether you pick them in the wild or buy them at the farmers' market, look for plump, juicy fresh blackberries or boysenberries for this pectin-free recipe. Macerating the berries with sugar overnight draws out their natural juices and helps produce a thick, intensely flavored jam.

MAKES ABOUT 6 (8-OUNCE) JARS

5 pounds fresh blackberries or boysenberries

4 cups granulated sugar

1/4 cup freshly squeezed lemon juice (about 1 lemon)

Rinse the berries in cool water. Transfer to a large glass bowl and combine with the sugar. Cover and refrigerate for at least 8 hours, or overnight, stirring occasionally to dissolve sugar and combine juices.

Prepare a water bath canner. Sterilize 6 half-pint jars, lids, and rings; keep them hot.

In a 6-quart Dutch oven or heavy-bottomed pot, warm the berry mixture over medium heat, stirring and breaking up berries with a spoon. When mixture is hot, remove from stove. Working in batches, press the mixture through a fine mesh sieve or food mill to remove the seeds.

Return the strained mixture back to the pot, add the lemon juice, and cook over medium-high heat until mixture comes to a boil. Boil, stirring often, until the temperature measures 220 degrees F on an instant-read thermometer, 5 to 8 minutes.

Remove from heat and skim off any foam, if necessary. Immediately ladle jam into hot jars, leaving 1/4-inch headspace. Wipe the rims of the jars with a damp paper towel. Tap the jars to remove any air bubbles, screw on the caps, and process them in the water bath canner for 15 minutes, or the time recommended for your area by your county extension agent. Cool the jars and press the top of each lid with a finger, ensuring the seal is tight and that the lid does not move up or down at all. (If any jars have not sealed properly, refrigerate them and eat the jam within 2 weeks.) Store sealed jars in a cool, dark place.

Grandma's Strawberry-Rhubarb Jam

Rhubarb and strawberries are two of the earliest fruits to ripen in late spring, and they are a classic flavor combination for this rosy-hued jam. Spread it on warm biscuits or scones for a delicious treat.

MAKES 7 (8-OUNCE) JARS

1 quart fresh strawberries, hulled

2 cups chopped fresh rhubarb

1/4 cup freshly squeezed lemon juice (about 1 lemon)

6 1/2 tablespoons classic powdered pectin

5 1/2 cups sugar

Prepare a water bath canner. Sterilize 7 half-pint jars, lids, and rings; keep them hot.

Spread the strawberries on a rimmed baking sheet and crush well with a potato masher or large, heavy metal spoon. Crush strawberries thoroughly, measure 2 cups crushed strawberries (save any leftover berries for another use), and pour into a 6-quart Dutch oven or large heavy-bottomed pot. Add the rhubarb, lemon juice, and pectin; stir to combine. Bring to a full rolling boil over high heat, stirring constantly. Stir in the sugar and return to a full rolling boil. Boil and stir for 1 minute. Remove from heat and skim off any foam, if necessary.

Immediately ladle jam into hot jars, leaving 1/4-inch headspace. Wipe the rims of the jars with a damp paper towel. Tap the jars to remove any air bubbles, screw on the caps, and process them in the water bath canner for 15 minutes, or the time recommended for your area by your county extension agent. Cool the jars and press the top of each lid with a finger, ensuring the seal is tight and that the lid does not move up or down at all. (If any jars have not sealed properly, refrigerate them and eat the jam within 2 weeks.) Store sealed jars in a cool, dark place.

Strawberry-Peach Preserves

If you make a batch of this pretty jam when peaches and strawberries are juicy and ripe, you can enjoy the taste of summertime any time you like.

MAKES 7 (8-OUNCE) JARS

1 quart fresh ripe strawberries, hulled

1½ pounds ripe peaches, peeled and pitted

2 tablespoons freshly squeezed lemon juice

4½ tablespoons classic powdered pectin

½ teaspoon unsalted butter

6 cups sugar

Prepare a water bath canner. Sterilize 7 half-pint jars, lids, and rings; keep them hot.

Spread the strawberries on a rimmed baking sheet and crush well with a potato masher or large, heavy metal spoon. Measure exactly 2¼ cups crushed strawberries (save any leftover berries for another use) and pour into a 6-quart Dutch oven or heavy-bottomed pot. Finely chop the peaches. Measure exactly 2 cups chopped peaches, add to the pot, and stir to blend. Add the lemon juice and stir to combine. Stir in the pectin and add butter to reduce foaming.

Over high heat, bring the mixture to a full rolling boil, stirring constantly. Add the sugar, stirring constantly. Return mixture to a full rolling boil. Boil for 1 minute, stirring constantly. Remove from heat and skim off any foam, if necessary.

Immediately ladle the preserves into hot jars, leaving ¼-inch headspace. Wipe the rims of the jars with a damp paper towel. Tap the jars to remove any air bubbles, screw on the caps, and process them in the water bath canner for 15 minutes, or the time recommended for your area by your county extension agent. Cool the jars and press the top of each lid with a finger, ensuring the seal is tight and that the lid does not move up or down at all. (If any jars have not sealed properly, refrigerate them and eat the preserves within 2 weeks.) Store sealed jars in a cool, dark place.

Whole Berry Cranberry Sauce

You may never buy canned sauce again after preparing a batch of this home-made cranberry sauce, which takes just 30 minutes to make. Perfect with roast turkey, the tangy topping also pairs nicely with pork chops, steaks, and fish.

MAKES ABOUT 2 1/4 CUPS, OR SERVES 6

1 cup cranberry juice

1/2 cup granulated sugar

1/2 cup honey

2 teaspoons lemon zest

1/8 teaspoon salt

1 (12-ounce) package fresh cranberries

Combine the juice, sugar, honey, lemon zest, and salt in a medium saucepan over medium-high heat. Bring to a boil, stirring frequently. Add the cranberries and return to a boil, stirring frequently.

Reduce heat to medium and cook for 10 minutes, stirring occasionally. Remove from heat, cover, and cool to room temperature. Serve or store in refrigerator, covered, for up to 3 days.

Homemade Blueberry Pancake Syrup

Overly sweet store-bought syrups can't compare to this homemade fruit-forward version. It's divine with waffles and pancakes or drizzled over cake or ice cream for an easy dessert.

MAKES ABOUT 2 1/4 CUPS

1 cup plus 2 tablespoons water, divided

1 tablespoon cornstarch

1/2 cup granulated sugar

1 tablespoon pure maple syrup

1/2 teaspoon vanilla extract

1/8 teaspoon salt

2 cups fresh or frozen (thawed and drained) blueberries

In a small dish, whisk together 2 tablespoons of the water and the cornstarch; reserve.

In a medium saucepan over medium-high heat, combine the remaining 1 cup water, sugar, maple syrup, vanilla, salt, and blueberries; stir until the sugar is dissolved. Bring to a boil, stirring occasionally. Reduce heat and simmer until slightly thickened, about 10 minutes.

Add the reserved cornstarch mixture and continue cooking, stirring constantly and crushing blueberries with the spoon, until sauce thickens.

Remove syrup from stove and cool for 5 minutes. Pour through a medium wire mesh strainer into a heatproof pitcher and serve at once. Refrigerate leftover syrup, covered, for up to 1 week.

Muffins,
Breads
&
Pastries

Blueberry Cinnamon-Streusel Muffins

Moist and rich, these bakery-style muffins are loaded with juicy blueberries and topped with crumbly streusel. They are equally delicious prepared with in-season or frozen blueberries.

MAKES 12 MUFFINS

1/4 cup firmly packed brown sugar

2 1/2 cups plus 1 tablespoon all-purpose flour, divided

1/2 cup plus 1 tablespoon unsalted butter, melted and cooled

1/8 teaspoon ground cinnamon

1/2 teaspoon salt, plus extra for topping

1 tablespoon baking powder

1 teaspoon baking soda

1 cup granulated sugar

2 large eggs

1 cup whole milk

2 teaspoons vanilla extract

1 1/2 cups fresh or frozen (thawed and drained) blueberries

Preheat the oven to 375 degrees F. Line a 12-cup muffin pan with paper liners.

In a small bowl, stir together the brown sugar, 1 tablespoon of the flour, 1 tablespoon of the butter, cinnamon, and a pinch of salt; reserve.

In a large bowl, whisk together the remaining 2 1/2 cups flour, baking powder, baking soda, and remaining 1/2 teaspoon salt; reserve. In a medium bowl, whisk the remaining 1/2 cup butter with the granulated sugar. Add the eggs, one at a time, whisking after each addition. Add the milk and vanilla and stir until combined. Add the milk mixture to the flour mixture and stir gently until just moistened. Fold in the blueberries until just incorporated; do not overmix.

Fill the muffin cups two-thirds full with the batter, top with streusel, and bake until a toothpick inserted into the center of a muffin comes out clean, 25 to 30 minutes. Cool muffins in pan for 10 minutes before removing to a wire rack.

Dutch Raspberry-Lemon Muffins

Lemon yogurt is the secret ingredient that gives these raspberry muffins a tender crumb and balanced flavor. The crispy topping is borrowed from a Dutch Apple Pie recipe.

MAKES 12 MUFFINS

2$\frac{1}{4}$ cups all-purpose flour, divided

$\frac{1}{2}$ cup granulated sugar

2 teaspoons baking powder

$\frac{1}{2}$ teaspoon baking soda

$\frac{1}{2}$ teaspoon salt

2 large eggs, lightly beaten

1 cup full-fat lemon yogurt

$\frac{1}{2}$ cup vegetable oil

1 teaspoon grated lemon peel

1 cup fresh or frozen (thawed and drained) raspberries

$\frac{1}{3}$ cup firmly packed light brown sugar

2 tablespoons salted butter

Preheat the oven to 400 degrees F. Grease a 12-cup muffin pan or line with paper liners.

In a large bowl, whisk together 2 cups of the flour, granulated sugar, baking powder, baking soda, and salt. In a medium bowl, whisk together the eggs, yogurt, oil, and lemon peel until well blended. Add the yogurt mixture to the flour mixture and stir just until moistened. Fold in the raspberries.

Fill prepared muffin cups three-fourths full. In a small bowl, combine the brown sugar and remaining $\frac{1}{4}$ cup flour. Cut in the butter until mixture resembles coarse crumbs; sprinkle about 1 tablespoon over each muffin. Bake until a toothpick inserted into the center of a muffin comes out clean, 18 to 20 minutes. Cool muffins in pan for 10 minutes before removing to a wire rack.

Strawberries and Cream Muffins

Are they muffins? Or cupcakes? No matter how you classify them, these breakfast treats starring the fresh flavor of strawberries with a lightly sweetened cream cheese filling are sure to please.

MAKES 16 TO 18 MUFFINS

3 cups all-purpose flour

1 tablespoon baking powder

1/2 teaspoon baking soda

1/4 teaspoon salt

1 1/4 cups milk

2 large eggs, lightly beaten

1 cup unsalted butter, melted

2 cups diced fresh strawberries

1 1/2 cups granulated sugar

8 ounces cream cheese, softened

1/2 cup powdered sugar

1/2 teaspoon vanilla extract

Preheat the oven to 375 degrees F. Line muffin pans with 18 paper liners.

In a large bowl, whisk together the flour, baking powder, baking soda, and salt. In a medium bowl, whisk together the milk, eggs, and melted butter. Make a well in the middle of the dry mixture, pour the wet mixture into the well, and stir until just combined; do not overmix. Add the strawberries and granulated sugar and stir gently to combine.

Spoon the batter into the prepared muffin cups about two-thirds full. Bake for 20 to 25 minutes, until a toothpick comes out clean and the tops are browned. Remove from oven and cool on a wire rack to room temperature.

In a small bowl, combine the cream cheese, powdered sugar, and vanilla; stir until smooth. Use a sharp paring knife to cut a cone-shaped core into the top of each muffin; eat or discard cores. Pipe or spoon 1 rounded tablespoon of filling into each hole. Serve immediately or store in the refrigerator for up to 2 days. Bring to room temperature before serving.

Blueberry Jelly Donuts

Delicious from the inside out, these yeast-raised jelly donuts will be the hit of any breakfast or brunch. They fry up light and crispy, and a homemade blueberry filling adds the ultimate fresh flavor.

MAKES ABOUT 18 DONUTS

---

2 tablespoons cornstarch

2 tablespoons water

2 cups fresh or frozen (thawed and drained) blueberries

1/3 cup plus 2 1/2 tablespoons granulated sugar, divided

1 teaspoon freshly squeezed lemon juice

1 cup warm water

4 1/2 teaspoons instant yeast

6 tablespoons unsalted butter, melted

1 large egg, beaten

1 teaspoon vanilla extract

3 1/2 cups all-purpose flour

1 teaspoon ground cinnamon

1 teaspoon ground nutmeg

1/2 teaspoon salt

Peanut oil, for frying

Powdered sugar, for sprinkling

Line a baking sheet with parchment paper and set aside.

In a small bowl, mix the cornstarch and water together until fully combined. In a heavy saucepan over medium heat, combine the blueberries, 1/3 cup of the sugar, and lemon juice; bring to a boil, stirring constantly. Add the cornstarch mixture and stir constantly until mixture bubbles and thickens. Remove from heat, cover, and reserve.

Combine the remaining 2 1/2 tablespoons sugar and warm water in a large bowl. Sprinkle with the yeast, stir gently, and let sit undisturbed for 5 minutes. Add the melted butter, egg, and vanilla; whisk to blend. In a medium bowl, whisk together the flour, cinnamon, nutmeg, and salt until well combined. Add the flour mixture to the butter mixture and stir to blend.

Transfer the dough to a lightly floured work surface and knead until smooth, about 2 minutes. Roll out the dough with a lightly floured rolling pin to a 1/2-inch thickness and cut 3-inch rounds with a lightly floured biscuit cutter; re-roll scraps and repeat. Transfer dough rounds to the prepared baking sheet and let rise in a warm area for 30 minutes.

Heat 2 inches of oil in a large heavy-bottomed saucepan to 360 degrees F. Fry the donuts 2 or 3 at a time, turning once so that both sides cook evenly. Use a slotted spoon to transfer cooked donuts to drain on paper towels.

Pour the blueberry filling into a pastry bag fitted with a large metal tip. Insert the tip $\frac{1}{2}$ inch into each donut and carefully pipe some of the filling inside. Sprinkle with powdered sugar and serve immediately.

Strawberry Sweet Rolls with Cream Cheese Frosting

There is nothing quite like the aroma of homemade sweet rolls right out of the oven. These yeast rolls are filled with strawberry jam and fresh strawberries then topped with a cream cheese frosting while they are still warm.

MAKES 12 ROLLS

1/4 cup granulated sugar

1/4 cup warm water

2 1/4 teaspoons or 1 (1/4-ounce) package dry yeast

1/4 cup milk

1/2 teaspoon salt

1 large egg

7 tablespoons unsalted butter, softened, divided

2 1/4 cups all-purpose flour

1/2 cup strawberry jam

1 quart fresh strawberries, chopped

1/2 cup cream cheese, softened

1 teaspoon vanilla extract

1–1 1/2 cups powdered sugar

In a small bowl, mix together 1/4 cup of the granulated sugar and the warm water. Add yeast and let sit undisturbed for 5 minutes.

Pour the yeast mixture into a large bowl and add the milk, salt, egg, and 4 tablespoons of the butter. Beat with an electric mixer on low speed. Add flour, increase speed to medium, and beat until dough comes together. Turn dough out onto a lightly floured work surface and knead until it becomes elastic, about 3 minutes. Lightly grease a bowl and transfer the dough to the bowl, turning once to coat. Cover with a damp towel and let rise for 1 hour.

Preheat the oven to 350 degrees F and grease a 9 x 13-inch baking pan.

Punch dough down, and then roll into a rectangle about 12 x 18 inches. Spread the jam evenly over the dough, and then distribute the chopped strawberries evenly. Roll up the long side of the dough like a jelly roll, pinching the seam. Use a serrated knife to cut the roll in half. Cut each half in 6 pieces.

Arrange rolls in prepared baking pan, cover with a damp towel, and let rise for 30 minutes. Remove towel and bake rolls until golden brown, 15 to 20 minutes.

While the rolls are baking, combine the cream cheese, remaining 3 tablespoons butter, and vanilla in a small bowl and stir to blend. Add enough powdered sugar to make a soft, spreadable icing. When rolls are finished baking, cool on a wire rack for 10 minutes and spread with the icing.

Blackberries 'n' Cream Pinwheels

These impressive pastries only *look* difficult to make. Flaky puff pastry pinwheels are anchored with a sweet, creamy filling and topped with blackberry jam, fresh berries, and sparkling sugar.

MAKES 8 PASTRIES

8 ounces cream cheese, softened

1/3 cup granulated sugar

2 teaspoons freshly squeezed lemon juice

1 teaspoon lemon zest

2 teaspoons vanilla extract

1 (17.3-ounce) package frozen puff pastry (2 sheets), thawed

1/2 cup blackberry jam

1 1/2 cups fresh blackberries or boysenberries

1 large egg

1 tablespoon water

Sparkling sugar, for sprinkling

Preheat the oven to 400 degrees F and line two baking sheets with parchment paper.

In a medium bowl, beat the cream cheese with an electric mixer on high speed until smooth. Add the sugar, lemon juice, lemon zest, and vanilla; beat until smooth. Reserve.

On a lightly floured work surface, roll out each sheet of thawed puff pastry to a 10-inch square. Cut each square into 4 equal squares and transfer to the prepared baking sheets, leaving 2 inches between each square. Prick the pastry squares with a fork. Spoon 1 heaping tablespoon of the cream cheese mixture into the center of each square, spreading in a small circle about 1 1/2 inches in diameter. Spoon 1 tablespoon of the jam on top of the cream cheese mixture and top with 4 blackberries.

Use a sharp knife to make 4 diagonal cuts from the corners of each pastry square to within 1 inch of the center. Fold every other corner up over the filling to the center, overlapping the points and pinching to seal.

In a small bowl, whisk together the egg and water. Brush each pinwheel all over with the egg wash. Sprinkle the pastry with sparkling sugar. Bake until golden brown, 15 to 18 minutes. Cool on a wire rack for 5 to 10 minutes before serving.

Blackberry Buttermilk Cornbread

Studded with blackberries and baked in a cast iron skillet until golden brown, this buttermilk-based cornbread is delicious on its own and also makes a perfect accompaniment to fried chicken, soups, and stews.

SERVES 8

8 tablespoons unsalted butter, melted, divided

1¼ cups all-purpose flour

½ cup cornmeal

1 teaspoon baking powder

¾ teaspoon salt

1¼ cups granulated sugar, divided

½ cup buttermilk

2 large eggs

12 ounces (about 3 cups) fresh or frozen (thawed and drained) blackberries

Preheat the oven to 375 degrees F. Brush the bottom and sides of a 9-inch cast iron skillet with 1 tablespoon of the butter and set aside.

In a medium bowl, whisk together the flour, cornmeal, baking powder, salt, and 1 cup plus 2 tablespoons of the sugar. In a large bowl, whisk together the buttermilk, eggs, and the remaining 7 tablespoons melted butter. Mix until combined. Add the flour mixture to the buttermilk mixture and stir just until moistened.

Pour the batter into the prepared skillet and sprinkle the blackberries evenly on top. Sprinkle with the remaining 2 tablespoons sugar.

Place the skillet on a baking sheet and bake until top of cornbread is golden brown and a toothpick inserted into the center comes out clean, 45 to 50 minutes. Cool on a wire rack for 30 minutes before cutting.

Raspberry Honey Scones

Raspberries add fresh summer flavor to these light, buttery scones sweetened with a hint of honey. They are delicious right out of the oven or spread with clotted cream and accompanied by a cup of tea.

MAKES 8 SCONES

1 cup fresh or frozen (thawed and drained) raspberries

2½ cups all-purpose flour, divided

1 tablespoon baking powder

6 tablespoons salted butter, chilled and cut into cubes

3/4 cup half-and-half

1/4 cup honey

1 large egg

Preheat the oven to 350 degrees F and line a baking sheet with parchment paper.

In a medium bowl, combine the raspberries with ½ cup of the flour and toss to blend; reserve.

In a medium bowl, whisk together the remaining 2 cups flour with the baking powder. Use two forks to cut in the butter until mixture resembles small peas; reserve.

In a small bowl, whisk together the half-and-half, honey, and egg until combined. Add to the flour mixture and stir until blended. Gently stir in the coated raspberries.

Place the dough on a lightly floured surface, knead a few times, and form into a round disc. With a lightly floured rolling pin, roll dough out into a 10-inch circle about 1 inch thick. Cut into 8 triangular sections then transfer to the prepared baking sheet. Bake scones until golden brown, about 10 minutes.

Heavenly Strawberry Banana Bread

This recipe updates the classic flavors of banana bread with fresh, juicy straw-berries. Simply sliced or toasted and buttered, this quick bread is great for breakfast or a snack.

MAKES 2 LOAVES

½ cup unsalted butter, softened

1 cup granulated sugar

2 large eggs, beaten

3 ripe bananas, mashed

1 teaspoon vanilla extract

2 cups plus 1 tablespoon all-purpose flour, divided

1 teaspoon baking soda

½ teaspoon salt

1½ cups roughly chopped fresh strawberries

Preheat the oven to 375 degrees F. Spray two 9 x 5-inch loaf pans with nonstick cooking spray and set aside.

In a large bowl, use an electric mixer to cream the butter and sugar together until light and fluffy. Add the eggs one at a time, beating after each addition. Add the bananas and vanilla and stir until combined. In a medium bowl, whisk together 2 cups of the flour, baking soda, and salt. Slowly add to banana mixture and stir just until moistened; do not overmix. In a small bowl, toss the strawberries with the remaining 1 tablespoon flour. Fold strawberries into the banana mixture just until combined.

Pour the batter into the prepared loaf pans and bake for 15 minutes. Reduce heat to 350 degrees F and continue baking for an additional 30 minutes, or until edges are lightly browned and a toothpick inserted into the center of each loaf comes out clean. Cool in pans for 15 minutes before turning out on a wire rack; cool completely before slicing and serving.

Salads
&
Starters

Warm Brie with Blueberry-Mango Salsa

A refreshing homemade fruit salsa perfectly complements the creamy, melty texture of Brie cheese in this easy appetizer recipe. Crispy homemade crostini provide the perfect base for the warm spread.

SERVES 12

3 tablespoons olive oil

3 tablespoons salted butter, melted

1 French baguette, cut diagonally into 1/2-inch slices

1 tablespoon freshly squeezed lime juice

2 teaspoons honey

1/4 teaspoon salt

1/2 cup fresh blueberries

1/2 cup diced mango

2 tablespoons minced red bell pepper

2 tablespoons minced red onion

1 tablespoon minced fresh cilantro

1 teaspoon finely minced jalapeño

1 (1-pound) round Brie cheese

Preheat the oven broiler to medium high and line a baking pan with aluminum foil. In a small bowl, combine the olive oil and butter. Brush the baguette slices with the mixture and arrange on the prepared baking pan. Broil until crispy and golden brown, 3 to 4 minutes. Remove from oven and transfer bread slices to a wire rack. Cool to room temperature and reserve.

In a small bowl, combine the lime juice, honey, and salt; whisk to combine. Add the blueberries, mango, bell pepper, onion, cilantro, and jalapeño. Stir gently to combine and reserve.

Preheat the oven to 400 degrees F.

Place the Brie in a round, shallow ovenproof casserole or cake pan no more than 2 inches wider than the cheese. Bake until cheese is melted in the center, 8 to 10 minutes. Remove from oven and spoon salsa on top. Serve warm with toasted baguette slices.

Roasted Green Bean Salad with Cranberry Vinaigrette and Toasted Pecans

In this simple salad, dried cranberries and crisp-tender green beans are a marriage made in heaven. Marinating the mix in homemade balsamic vinaigrette and lemon juice adds tangy flavor.

SERVES 8

½ cup roughly chopped pecans

2 pounds fresh green beans, trimmed

4 cloves garlic, peeled and sliced into quarters

2 tablespoons extra virgin olive oil

1¼ teaspoons sea salt

½ teaspoon freshly ground black pepper

2 teaspoons balsamic vinegar

1 teaspoon freshly squeezed lemon juice

½ cup dried cranberries

1 teaspoon freshly grated lemon zest

Preheat the oven to 350 degrees F. Spread the pecans on a rimmed baking sheet and bake, stirring once, until fragrant and lightly toasted, about 10 minutes. Remove from oven, cool on pan for 5 minutes, and transfer to a small dish; reserve.

Increase the oven temperature to 450 degrees F and line the baking sheet with heavy-duty aluminum foil. In a large bowl, toss the green beans with the garlic, olive oil, salt, and pepper. Spread on the prepared baking sheet. Roast the beans for 15 minutes,

remove from oven, and stir. Return to oven and continue roasting until beans are tender and just starting to brown, about 10 minutes more.

Remove from oven and cool to room temperature. Transfer the beans to a serving dish. Drizzle with the balsamic vinegar and lemon juice and toss well. Cover and refrigerate until chilled, about 2 hours. Sprinkle with the cranberries, lemon zest, and reserved pecans, and toss well. Adjust seasonings if necessary and serve immediately.

Spring Greens with Blackberries, Gorgonzola, and Walnuts

For this elegant restaurant-inspired salad, tender greens and sweet berries are tossed with crumbled creamy Gorgonzola cheese. Blueberry-balsamic vinaigrette highlights the salad's bright, fresh flavors, and toasted walnuts add texture and crunch.

SERVES 8

1/2 cup roughly chopped walnuts

3 tablespoons blueberry or raspberry vinegar

3 tablespoons balsamic vinegar

3 tablespoons extra virgin olive oil

1/4 teaspoon sea salt

1/4 teaspoon freshly ground black pepper

6 cups mixed spring greens

2 cups fresh blackberries

4 ounces crumbled Gorgonzola cheese

Place the walnuts in a skillet over medium heat and cook, stirring frequently, until fragrant and lightly browned, 5 to 6 minutes. Remove from heat and cool to room temperature; reserve.

In a small bowl, whisk together the blueberry or raspberry vinegar, balsamic vinegar, olive oil, salt, and pepper.

In a large bowl, combine the greens, blackberries, and Gorgonzola. Drizzle with the dressing mixture and toss gently to combine. Sprinkle with the reserved walnuts.

Strawberry Chicken Salad

Perfect for a luncheon or shower, this composed salad is as pretty on the plate as it is good to eat. With an appealing mix of fresh strawberries, greens, pears, avocados, and grilled chicken, it is substantial enough to star as a main dish.

SERVES 8

1 quart fresh strawberries, sliced, divided

1 cup Italian vinaigrette

4 boneless, skinless chicken breast halves

8 cups mixed salad greens

2 pears, sliced

2 avocados, sliced

1/2 small sweet onion, diced

Salt and freshly ground black pepper

1/2 cup chopped pecans, toasted

In a food processor or blender, purée 1/2 cup of the strawberries. Transfer mixture to a small bowl and whisk in the vinaigrette. Pour half of the mixture into a large zip-lock freezer bag. Reserve the other half of the mixture and refrigerate. Add the chicken to the zip-lock bag, toss to coat, and seal. Refrigerate for 1 hour.

Preheat the grill to medium-high heat (350 to 400 degrees F). Remove the chicken from the bag and discard the marinade. Arrange the chicken on the grill, cover, and cook until an instant-read thermometer inserted into the thickest part of the breast measures 160 degrees F, about 4 minutes on each side. Remove chicken from grill and let rest for 10 minutes; slice.

Combine the salad greens, remaining sliced strawberries, pears, avocados, and onion in a large bowl and gently toss. Divide mixture evenly between 8 chilled salad plates and top with grilled chicken slices. Drizzle with remaining strawberry vinaigrette and sprinkle with salt and pepper to taste; garnish with chopped pecans.

Blueberry and Butter Lettuce Salad with Oranges and Avocado

Sweet berries and oranges, creamy avocados, and crunchy toasted almonds create a delightful contrast with tender butter lettuce leaves in this delicious salad. A homemade dressing of champagne vinegar and Dijon mustard adds a zesty finish.

SERVES 8

½ cup slivered almonds

3 tablespoons granulated sugar

1 teaspoon Dijon mustard

1 teaspoon minced fresh garlic

3 tablespoons champagne vinegar

½ teaspoon sea salt

¼ teaspoon freshly ground black pepper

½ cup extra virgin olive oil

1 small head butter lettuce, torn into bite-sized pieces

1 small head romaine lettuce, torn into bite-sized pieces

2 cups fresh blueberries

1 (15-ounce) can mandarin oranges, drained

2 avocados, cubed

Line a baking sheet with aluminum foil and set aside. Combine the almonds and sugar in a medium skillet over medium-high heat; cook and stir until sugar is melted and coats almonds, 3 to 4 minutes. Spread almonds in a single layer on the prepared pan to cool. Reserve.

To make the salad dressing, whisk together the mustard, garlic, vinegar, salt, and pepper in a small bowl. While whisking, slowly add the olive oil until the mixture is emulsified. Reserve.

In a large bowl, gently toss together the butter lettuce, romaine lettuce, blueberries, oranges, and avocados. Sprinkle with candied almonds. Just before serving, whisk the dressing and drizzle over the salad; toss gently.

Cranberry-Glazed Meatballs

Whole berry cranberry sauce is the surprise ingredient that gives these tender appetizer meatballs pizzazz. The meatballs and sauce can be prepared ahead and served in a slow cooker or warming dish for parties and gatherings.

SERVES 24

2 pounds ground chuck

2 large eggs

1/3 cup dry breadcrumbs

1 teaspoon salt

1/2 teaspoon freshly ground black pepper

1/2 teaspoon garlic powder

1/2 teaspoon onion powder

1 (12-ounce) bottle chili sauce

1 3/4 cups Whole Berry Cranberry Sauce (page 32), or 1 (14-ounce) can whole berry cranberry sauce

1/4 cup marmalade

In a large bowl, combine the chuck, eggs, breadcrumbs, salt, pepper, garlic powder, and onion powder. Shape mixture into about 48 balls that are 1 inch in diameter.

In a large skillet over medium-high heat, cook meatballs in batches, turning occasionally, until browned on all sides, 5 to 7 minutes. Remove from pan with a slotted spoon and drain well on paper towels.

Stir together the chili sauce, cranberry sauce, and marmalade in a large Dutch oven or heavy pot over medium heat; cook for 5 minutes, whisking occasionally, or until smooth. Add meatballs, reduce heat to low, and cook, stirring occasionally, until centers are no longer pink, about 20 minutes. Serve warm with toothpicks.

Melon-Berry Mélange

This colorful, refreshing summer salad is a perfect light side dish for your next picnic or cookout. Lightly drizzled with a homemade honey-lemon dressing, it is simply garnished with a kiss of fresh mint.

SERVES 8

½ watermelon, scooped into balls to make about 2 cups

1 cantaloupe, scooped into balls to make about 2 cups

1 cup fresh blueberries

1 cup sliced fresh strawberries

⅓ cup honey

¼ cup freshly squeezed lemon juice (about 1 lemon)

¼ cup chopped fresh mint leaves

In a large bowl, combine the watermelon, cantaloupe, blueberries, and strawberries.

In a small bowl, whisk together the honey and lemon juice. Drizzle the dressing over the fruit mixture and stir gently to combine. Sprinkle with the chopped mint and stir gently. Serve at once or cover and refrigerate for up to 2 hours before serving.

Crown Ruby Salad

Satisfy your summer fruit cravings with a jeweled salad that pairs juicy watermelon with fresh red raspberries and ripe strawberries. A simple lime dressing and a sprinkle of fresh mint are the only adornments needed.

SERVES 8

3 tablespoons granulated sugar

3 tablespoons water

1 teaspoon freshly squeezed lime juice

1 teaspoon lime zest

1 pound fresh strawberries, halved

3 cups cubed watermelon ($\frac{1}{2}$-inch cubes)

1 (6-ounce) package fresh raspberries

1 tablespoon chopped fresh mint leaves

In a small saucepan, combine the sugar, water, lime juice, and lime zest. Heat over medium-high heat, stirring often, until mixture comes to a rolling boil. Remove from heat and cool, uncovered, to room temperature; reserve.

In a large serving bowl, combine the strawberries, watermelon, raspberries, and mint. Drizzle with lime syrup and toss gently until evenly coated. Serve immediately.

Main
Courses

Grilled Pork Tenderloin with Cranberry Balsamic Glaze

Pork tenderloin is fast and easy to grill, and its short cooking time keeps the meat juicy and flavorful. Topped with a glaze that pairs whole cranberries with zesty balsamic vinegar, this preparation is perfect for an elegant dinner party or a casual weekday dinner.

SERVES 4 TO 6

2/3 cup fresh or frozen (thawed and drained) cranberries

1/3 cup balsamic vinegar

2 tablespoons water

1 tablespoon honey

2 cloves garlic, minced

1 (1 1/2-pound) pork tenderloin

1/2 teaspoon salt

1/2 teaspoon freshly ground black pepper

1 teaspoon garlic powder

Combine the cranberries, balsamic vinegar, water, honey, and garlic in a medium saucepan. Bring to a boil over medium heat. Reduce heat to medium low and simmer, stirring occasionally, until thickened, about 30 minutes; reserve.

Preheat the grill to medium heat (300 to 350 degrees F) and oil the grill rack.

Season the pork tenderloin with salt, pepper, and garlic powder. Arrange the tenderloin on the grill and cook, turning frequently, until seared on all sides, about 5 minutes total. Brush pork with half of the cranberry glaze and cook, turning frequently, until an instant-read thermometer inserted into the center measures 150 degrees F. Remove pork from grill, tent with aluminum foil, and let rest for 5 minutes. Carve in slices against the grain and serve with remaining sauce.

Sticky Raspberry Barbecued Spare Ribs

Whole raspberries and raspberry jam impart bright berry notes to the barbecue sauce that enlivens these tender ribs. After slow cooking in the oven to bring out their hearty flavor, the ribs are finished on the grill and basted with extra sauce. Serve accompanied by plenty of extra napkins!

SERVES 4

1 cup fresh or frozen (thawed and drained) raspberries

1 cup raspberry jam

2/3 cup granulated sugar

2 1/2 cups prepared honey barbeque sauce

2 (2-pound) racks baby back pork ribs

Salt and freshly ground black pepper

Preheat the oven to 300 degrees F. Place a length of aluminum foil longer than the ribs on a heavy rimmed baking sheet.

To make the sauce, combine the raspberries, jam, and sugar in a medium saucepan. Cook over medium heat, mashing raspberries with a spoon, until sugar dissolves, about 5 minutes. Add the barbeque sauce and stir to combine. Continue cooking for 5 minutes. Remove from heat.

Sprinkle the ribs on both sides with salt and pepper and arrange skin side up on the prepared foil. Brush both sides of the ribs with the sauce. Cover ribs with another length of foil and fold edges tightly to seal. Bake until ribs are tender, about 2 hours. Refrigerate extra sauce in a covered container.

Preheat the grill to medium-high heat (350 to 400 degrees F) and oil the grate.

Remove the ribs from the oven and let rest for 10 minutes. Carefully unseal foil and transfer rib racks to a platter. Brush one side of the ribs generously with the reserved sauce. Lay the ribs sauce side down on the grill, and then brush the other side with the sauce. Put the lid down and cook each side for 4 to 5 minutes, just until browned. Remove to a cutting board and use a sharp knife to cut between each rib. Brush ribs with extra sauce and serve.

Grilled Halibut with Lemon-Blueberry Pan Sauce

Light, mild halibut is the perfect foil for a citrusy sauce with fresh ginger and blueberries. Rubbing the fillets with olive oil before grilling seals in juices and keeps the fish moist and flaky.

SERVES 4

Juice of 1 lemon

1 tablespoon cornstarch

1½ cups fresh or frozen (thawed and drained) blueberries

3 tablespoons honey

⅛ teaspoon ground ginger

4 (6-ounce) halibut fillets

1 tablespoon olive oil

½ teaspoon salt

½ teaspoon freshly ground black pepper

Zest of ½ lemon, for garnish

Preheat the grill to medium heat (300 to 350 degrees F) and lightly oil the grate.

In a medium saucepan, combine the lemon juice and cornstarch and whisk to blend. Add the blueberries, honey, and ginger; stir to combine. Heat over medium-high heat, stirring frequently, until mixture thickens and just starts to bubble, about 5 minutes. Reduce heat to low, cover, and keep warm.

Rub both sides of the halibut fillets with olive oil and sprinkle with salt and pepper. Arrange on the grill and cook, turning once, until fish flakes easily when tested with a fork, 3 to 4 minutes per side. Serve topped with blueberry sauce and garnished with lemon zest.

Cranberry Brined and Glazed Roast Turkey Breast

Brining is an easy step that helps a bone-in turkey breast stay moist during cooking. This simple brine has the added benefit of lending a complex cranberry-apple flavor to the meat. A homemade cranberry glaze seals in juices while roasting and is the perfect accompaniment to the tender sliced turkey.

SERVES 8

$4\frac{1}{2}$ cups apple cider, divided

$2\frac{1}{2}$ cups cranberry juice, divided

$\frac{1}{2}$ cup kosher salt

$\frac{1}{4}$ cup firmly packed dark brown sugar

2 tablespoons pickling spice blend

1 teaspoon red pepper flakes

Ice and water

1 (4-pound) skin-on, bone-in turkey breast

2 cups fresh or frozen (thawed and drained) cranberries

$\frac{1}{2}$ cup maple syrup

$\frac{1}{2}$ cup apple cider vinegar

Salt and freshly ground black pepper

Extra virgin olive oil

To make the brine, combine $2\frac{1}{2}$ cups of the apple cider, $1\frac{1}{2}$ cups of the cranberry juice, kosher salt, brown sugar, pickling spice, and red pepper flakes in a large stockpot or Dutch oven. Bring to a simmer over medium-high heat and cook, stirring occasionally, until the salt and sugar have dissolved and the spices are fragrant, 35 to 40 minutes. When the mixture is almost done cooking, combine ice and water in a pitcher to make 8 cups. Remove the pot from the stove and cool for 5 minutes. Add the ice water and stir until ice melts.

Place the turkey breast skin side down into a large bowl and pour the brine over the top. Cover and refrigerate for 4 hours, turning turkey breast several times to distribute brine.

To make the glaze, combine the remaining 2 cups apple cider, remaining 1 cup cranberry juice, cranberries, maple syrup, and apple cider vinegar in a medium saucepan. Bring to a boil over medium-high heat. Reduce to medium-low heat and simmer until the liquid has been reduced by about 2 cups and the cranberries break down, 18 to 20 minutes. Remove from heat and cool to room temperature. Season to taste with salt and pepper. Transfer mixture to a blender or food processor and purée until smooth; reserve.

Preheat the oven to 350 degrees F and place a rack in a roasting pan.

Remove the turkey breast from the brine, pat dry with paper towels, and place skin side up in roasting pan. Rub the turkey breast all over with olive oil and sprinkle with pepper. Roast until the breast reaches an internal temperature of 160 degrees F, about 1 hour and 40 minutes, brushing with the cranberry mixture every 10 to 15 minutes. Remove the turkey breast from the oven and tent with aluminum foil. Let rest for 10 to 15 minutes before carving. Serve accompanied with remaining glaze.

Grilled Flank Steak with Blackberry Sauce

Flank steak cooks up quickly and easily on the grill thanks to a garlicky marinade that tenderizes the meat and imparts flavor. After slicing the steak thinly on the diagonal, it is served with a vibrant blackberry sauce.

SERVES 6

1/2 cup vegetable oil

1/3 cup low-sodium soy sauce

1/4 cup red wine vinegar

2 tablespoons freshly squeezed lime juice

1 1/2 tablespoons Worcestershire sauce

1 tablespoon Dijon mustard

2 cloves garlic, minced

1/2 teaspoon freshly ground black pepper, plus more for seasoning

2 pounds flank steak

4 tablespoons cold unsalted butter, divided

2 shallots, finely chopped

1 cup red wine

1 1/3 cups beef stock or low-sodium beef broth

1/2 cup fresh or frozen (thawed and drained) blackberries

1/4 cup blackberry jam or preserves

Salt

Chopped fresh mint leaves, for garnish

In a medium bowl, whisk together the oil, soy sauce, vinegar, lime juice, Worcestershire sauce, Dijon mustard, garlic, and pepper. Place the flank steak in a shallow glass dish. Pour marinade over the steak, turning meat to coat thoroughly. Cover and refrigerate for at least 6 hours, or overnight, turning steak several times to distribute marinade.

Preheat the grill to medium-high heat (350 to 400 degrees F) and oil the grate. Remove steak from marinade and arrange on the grill, discarding marinade. Grill meat for about 5 minutes per side, or to desired doneness. Transfer to a cutting board, tent with aluminum foil, and allow to rest for 10 minutes before slicing thinly across the grain.

While the steak is resting, melt 2 tablespoons of the butter in a large saucepan over medium heat. Add the shallots and cook until softened, 3 to 4 minutes. Add the wine and increase the heat to medium high.

Bring to a boil and cook until wine is reduced by half, 3 to 5 minutes. Add the beef stock, blackberries, and jam. Stir, mashing the berries with the spoon. Bring to a simmer and cook until the sauce is thickened, 4 to 5 minutes.

Remove sauce from heat and stir in the remaining 2 tablespoons butter. Season to taste with salt and pepper. To serve, drizzle sliced flank steak with blackberry sauce and sprinkle with fresh mint.

Grilled Chicken with Raspberry Balsamic Sauce

An easy one-pan dinner begins with a sweet and savory reduction sauce that pairs raspberries with balsamic vinegar and red wine. Chicken breasts are grilled to perfection before being drizzled with the sauce and topped with whole raspberries.

SERVES 4

4 teaspoons extra virgin olive oil, divided

2 large shallots, sliced

1 clove garlic, minced

3 cups fresh raspberries, divided

2 tablespoons balsamic vinegar

1/3 cup red wine

3/4 cup chicken broth

1 1/2 teaspoons cornstarch

2 teaspoons cold water

Salt and freshly ground black pepper

4 (5- to 6-ounce) boneless, skinless chicken breasts

To make the sauce, heat 2 teaspoons of the oil in a medium saucepan over medium-high heat. Add the shallots and garlic and cook until fragrant and lightly browned, about 2 minutes. Reserve 1/4 cup of the raspberries for garnish. Add the remaining 2 3/4 cups raspberries to the pan and cook for 3 minutes, stirring constantly and breaking up the berries with a spoon to release the juice. Add the vinegar, wine, and broth; bring to a simmer. Cook, stirring occasionally, until mixture is reduced by half. In a small dish, whisk the cornstarch and water together. Add mixture to the saucepan and cook, stirring, until mixture is thickened, 2 to 3 more minutes. Pour sauce through a wire mesh strainer into a clean container. Return the sauce to the saucepan, season to taste with salt and pepper, cover, and reserve.

Preheat the grill to medium-high heat (350 to 400 degrees F).

Coat the chicken with the remaining 2 teaspoons oil and sprinkle both sides with salt and pepper. Cook on the grill until marks form, about 4 minutes. Flip chicken and continue cooking for about 4 more minutes, until an instant-read thermometer inserted in the thickest part measures 160 degrees F. Transfer to a serving platter, drizzle with the sauce, and garnish with reserved raspberries.

Boysenberry-Ginger Glazed Salmon

Quick-broiled salmon fillets could not be simpler to prepare in this Asian-inspired recipe. Fresh ginger, lemon juice, and sweet boysenberries combine for a fast and flavorful sauce, and this company-worthy dinner can be ready to serve in under 45 minutes.

SERVES 4

1 tablespoon extra virgin olive oil, divided

1 cup water

12 ounces fresh or frozen (thawed and drained) boysenberries

1 (1-inch) fresh ginger root, peeled and thinly sliced

Juice of 1/2 lemon

1/4 cup firmly packed brown sugar

4 (8-ounce) skinless salmon fillets

Salt and freshly ground black pepper

Preheat the oven to 400 degrees F. Brush a heavy rimmed baking sheet with 1/2 tablespoon of the olive oil; set aside.

In a small saucepan over medium-high heat, combine the water, boysen-berries, ginger, and lemon juice. Bring to a boil, reduce to a simmer, and cook until berries break down, about 5 minutes. Remove berries from heat and strain into a container, pushing on the solids. Discard solids and return the mixture to the saucepan. Add the brown sugar and cook over medium-high heat, stirring frequently, until brown sugar is dissolved and mixture comes to a boil. Reduce heat to medium low and simmer, stirring often, until reduced by half. Remove from heat and cool mixture to room temperature.

Arrange salmon fillets on the prepared baking sheet, brush with remaining 1/2 tablespoon olive oil, and sprinkle on both sides with salt and pepper. Brush cooled boysenberry mixture over salmon fillets and bake for 4 minutes. Remove from oven and turn broiler on. Turn fillets over and brush generously with boysenberry mixture. Return to oven and broil until sauce bubbles and fillets are lightly browned, about 3 minutes.

Blackberry-Glazed Spiral Ham

Spiral-sliced ham is a great way to feed a crowd, and since it is precooked, it is quick to prepare. Your guests will love the way this honey-blackberry glaze cooks into the meat and imparts sweet, tangy flavor that complements the salty ham.

SERVES 10 TO 12

1 (6- to 7-pound) cooked bone-in spiral-sliced ham, liquid reserved

1 cup orange juice

1/2 cup seedless blackberry jam

1 cup fresh blackberries or boysenberries, plus more for garnish

1/2 cup honey

1 teaspoon red pepper flakes

Preheat the oven to 325 degrees F. Place a rack in a roasting pan and set aside.

To make the glaze, combine the reserved ham liquid, orange juice, jam, blackberries, honey, and red pepper flakes in a medium saucepan. Bring to a boil over medium-high heat. Reduce heat to medium low and simmer, stirring occasionally, until mixture thickens, 15 to 20 minutes. Remove from heat and reserve.

Place the ham in the prepared roasting pan, spiral slices up. Brush generously with the glaze and cover loosely with aluminum foil. Bake, brushing every 15 minutes with the glaze, until ham is hot and an instant-read thermometer measures 140 degrees F, about 2 hours or 20 minutes per pound.

Remove the ham from the oven and increase temperature to 425 degrees F. Remove foil from ham and spoon remaining glaze generously over the top and sides. Bake until top of ham is crispy and heated through, about 10 minutes more. Remove from oven and let rest for 10 minutes before slicing. Serve garnished with fresh blackberries.

Strawberry Sweet and Sour Chicken

Why buy takeout when you can whip up this winning Chinese restaurant favorite in short order in your own kitchen? The tangy sauce accompanying the crispy, flash-fried chicken gets its vibrant color and flavor from fresh strawberries.

SERVES 6

---

2 tablespoons low-sodium soy sauce

2 tablespoons rice wine or white wine

1 tablespoon cornstarch

2 pounds boneless, skinless chicken thighs, cut into 1-inch cubes

1/3 cup strawberry jam

1/4 cup orange juice

2 teaspoons balsamic vinegar

1 teaspoon freshly squeezed lemon juice

2 tablespoons peanut oil

1 teaspoon minced garlic

1 teaspoon minced ginger

1/2 cup sliced fresh strawberries

Salt and freshly ground black pepper

Hot cooked rice, for serving

In a medium bowl, combine the soy sauce, rice wine, and cornstarch. Add the chicken and marinate for 15 minutes, turning several times to coat.

In a small saucepan, combine the strawberry jam, orange juice, balsamic vinegar, and lemon juice. Heat over medium heat, stirring often, until jam melts and mixture is smooth. Cover and reserve.

Heat the oil in a wok or heavy skillet over medium-high heat. When oil shimmers, add the minced garlic and ginger; cook, stirring constantly, for 15 seconds. Add the chicken and its marinade; cook, stirring constantly and separating chicken pieces, until chicken is lightly browned and cooked through, about 5 minutes. Use a slotted spoon to remove the chicken to drain on paper towels.

Add the strawberries to the hot pan and stir-fry for 30 seconds. Add the reserved sauce and cook, stirring constantly, until hot, about 1 minute. Add the chicken back to the pan and cook, stirring constantly, until the chicken is coated with sauce and cooked through. Season to taste with salt and pepper. Serve immediately over hot rice.

Cakes
&
Cookies

Blueberry Swirl Pound Cake

A sour cream–based batter creates a tender crumb in this fresh take on an old-fashioned pound cake. When the cake is cut, each slice shows off a pretty swirl of blueberry.

MAKES 1 LOAF

1/2 cup unsalted butter, at room temperature, plus extra for greasing pan

1 cup fresh or frozen (thawed and drained) blueberries

1 1/4 cups plus 2 tablespoons granulated sugar, divided

1 1/2 cups all-purpose flour

1/2 teaspoon salt

1/4 teaspoon baking powder

2 large eggs, lightly beaten

1/2 teaspoon vanilla extract

1/2 cup sour cream, at room temperature

Preheat the oven to 350 degrees F. Lightly butter a 9 x 5-inch loaf pan and line with parchment paper, leaving a 2-inch overhang on long sides; butter the parchment paper.

In a food processor or blender, purée the blueberries with 2 tablespoons of the sugar and reserve. In a medium bowl, whisk together the flour, salt, and baking powder. In a large bowl, combine the butter with the remaining 1 1/4 cups sugar and beat with an electric mixer on medium-high speed until light and fluffy, about 5 minutes. Add the eggs and vanilla and beat until combined. With mixer on low, add flour mixture in three additions, alternating with the sour cream.

Transfer half of the batter to the prepared pan. Spoon half of the blueberry puree in dollops over the batter. Repeat with the remaining batter and purée. With a thin-bladed knife, gently swirl the batter and blueberry mixture. Bake until golden brown and a toothpick inserted into the center of the cake comes out clean, about 1 hour 25 minutes. Let cool in pan on a wire rack for 30 minutes. Lift cake out of pan and cool completely before slicing.

Lemon-Glazed Mixed Berry Bundt Cake

A sunny lemon Bundt cake will brighten anyone's day, especially when it is filled with a mixture of berries. The buttermilk-based batter creates a cake that is moist and tender, and it is topped with a generous drizzle of sweet, tangy honey-lemon glaze.

SERVES 10

2$\frac{3}{4}$ cups plus 1 tablespoon all-purpose flour, divided

1$\frac{1}{2}$ teaspoons baking powder

$\frac{1}{4}$ teaspoon baking soda

$\frac{1}{4}$ teaspoon salt

1 cup unsalted butter, softened

1$\frac{3}{4}$ cups granulated sugar

4 large eggs

4 tablespoons freshly squeezed lemon juice, divided

1 tablespoon lemon zest, plus extra for garnish

1 teaspoon vanilla extract

1 cup buttermilk

1$\frac{1}{4}$ cups mixed fresh or frozen (thawed and drained) berries

1$\frac{1}{2}$ cups powdered sugar

1 tablespoon honey

Preheat the oven to 350 degrees F. Spray a 12-cup Bundt pan with nonstick cooking spray.

In a medium bowl, whisk together 2$\frac{3}{4}$ cups of the flour, baking powder, baking soda, and salt; reserve. In a large bowl, combine the butter and sugar and beat with an electric mixer on medium speed until fluffy, 2 to 3 minutes. Beat in the eggs, one at a time, mixing well after each addition. Add 2 tablespoons of the lemon juice, lemon zest, and vanilla; beat until combined. Beat in the flour mixture in three additions, alternating with buttermilk and beating until smooth.

In a medium bowl, combine the berries with the remaining 1 tablespoon flour. Fold the berries into the batter. Spoon batter into the prepared Bundt pan. Bake until a toothpick inserted into the center of the cake comes out clean, about 50 minutes. Cool in pan on a wire rack for 20 minutes. Run a sharp knife around the edges of the pan. Turn the cake out and cool completely.

While the cake is cooling, combine the powdered sugar, the remaining 2 tablespoons lemon juice, and honey in a small bowl; stir until smooth.

Transfer the cooled cake to a serving platter, and then drizzle the glaze over the top and sides of cake. Garnish with lemon zest.

Huckleberry Buckle

As fun to say as it is to eat, this recipe begins with an extra-rich butter-based crust. Next, fresh huckleberries are scattered artfully on top. Finally, the berries are covered with a light, crumbly topping and baked to bubbly, buckle-y perfection. If you have difficulty finding huckleberries, you can substitute blueberries.

SERVES 8

---

1 cup unsalted butter, softened, divided

1 cup granulated sugar, divided

1 large egg

$2\frac{1}{2}$ cups all-purpose flour, divided

$2\frac{1}{2}$ teaspoons baking powder

$\frac{1}{4}$ teaspoon salt

$\frac{3}{4}$ cup sour cream

2 pints fresh huckleberries

$\frac{1}{2}$ cup all-purpose flour

$\frac{3}{4}$ teaspoon ground cinnamon

Preheat the oven to 375 degrees F and grease an 8 x 8-inch glass baking dish.

In a large bowl, combine $\frac{1}{2}$ cup of the butter and $\frac{1}{2}$ cup of the sugar and beat with an electric mixer until light and fluffy, 1 to 2 minutes. Add the egg and beat until combined. In a medium bowl, whisk together 2 cups of the flour, the baking powder, and salt. Beat the flour mixture into the butter mixture one-third at a time, alternating with the sour cream and beating well after each addition. Spread the batter into the prepared pan. Sprinkle the berries evenly over the batter.

To make the topping, combine remaining $\frac{1}{2}$ cup butter, $\frac{1}{2}$ cup sugar, $\frac{1}{2}$ cup flour, and the cinnamon in a medium bowl. Using your hands or two forks, cut the mixture together until it resembles coarse crumbs. Sprinkle over the berries.

Bake the buckle until the topping is puffed and browned, about 1 hour. Remove from oven and cool in the dish for 10 minutes on a wire rack. Serve warm.

Blueberry Almond Cake

This moist, dense, golden cake is short on prep time but long on flavor. Fresh blueberries are suspended in the rich, buttery batter and topped with crunchy almonds. Start the oven now, and you will be eating cake in an hour!

SERVES 6

½ cup unsalted butter, softened

1 cup granulated sugar

2 large eggs

½ teaspoon vanilla extract

½ teaspoon almond extract

1 teaspoon baking powder

¼ teaspoon salt

1 cup all-purpose flour

1 cup fresh blueberries

¼ cup sliced almonds

Preheat the oven to 350 degrees F and generously grease a 9-inch round cake pan.

In a large bowl with an electric mixer on high speed, beat the butter and sugar together until light and fluffy, about 2 minutes. Add the eggs one at a time, beating well after each addition. Add the vanilla and almond extracts and stir until combined.

In a medium bowl, whisk together the baking powder, salt, and flour. Fold the flour mixture into the butter mixture just until combined. Fold in the blueberries.

Spread the batter in the prepared pan. Sprinkle the sliced almonds on top and bake until a toothpick inserted into the center comes out clean, 25 to 30 minutes. Serve warm.

Strawberry Surprise Cupcakes

Perfect for strawberry lovers, these light and airy cupcakes are frosted with a dreamy pink strawberry whipped cream topping. Take a bite and you will discover true berry bliss—a fresh, juicy ripe strawberry tucked inside.

MAKES 18 CUPCAKES

1 (18.25-ounce*) box white cake mix

1 1/3 cups water

3 large egg whites

2 tablespoons unsalted butter, melted

2 teaspoons vanilla extract, divided

1 teaspoon almond extract

24 medium-sized fresh strawberries, divided

1 cup heavy whipping cream

1/3 cup powdered sugar

Preheat the oven to 350 degrees F. Line 18 muffin cups with paper liners.

Combine the cake mix, water, egg whites, butter, 1 teaspoon of the vanilla, and almond extract in a large bowl; beat with an electric mixer on high speed until well blended, about 2 minutes. Spoon the batter evenly into the prepared muffin cups.

Bake the cupcakes until lightly browned and a toothpick inserted into the center comes out clean, 15 to 20 minutes. Cool the cupcakes in the pan for 2 minutes. Remove from pan, transfer to a wire rack, and finish cooling to room temperature. Using a sharp knife, cut a 1-inch-round by 1-inch-deep core from each cupcake; reserve cores. Quarter 1 strawberry lengthwise, reassemble it,

and carefully insert it into the center of a cupcake. Repeat with remaining strawberries and cupcakes. Trim the cupcake cores to fit over the strawberries and replace on top of cupcakes, covering the strawberries.

Put the remaining 6 strawberries in a blender and purée; reserve. In a large bowl, combine the whipping cream and powdered sugar and beat with an electric mixer until stiff peaks form. Fold in the puréed strawberries. Frost the cupcakes with the strawberry cream and serve immediately. Refrigerate any leftover cupcakes.

Cake mix sizes change frequently. If your mix contains less than 18.25 ounces, you can add additional all-purpose flour to make up for the difference.

If you have a kitchen scale, simply weigh out the difference between your mix and 18.25 ounces. No scale? No problem. In volume, 1 ounce of flour equals 3.63 tablespoons, or a scant 1 tablespoon per .25 ounce. Measure the difference, add the flour to the bowl when you add the cake mix, and proceed as usual.

Blackberry Lemon Bars

What could be better than a classic lemon bar? Try a sweet-tart bar with a buttery shortbread crust and homemade lemon filling blanketed with a sticky-sweet blackberry sauce and baked to perfection.

MAKES 24 BARS

1 cup unsalted butter, softened

3½ cups plus 2 tablespoons granulated sugar, divided

2 tablespoons plus 1 teaspoon fresh lemon zest, divided

3 cups all-purpose flour, divided

¼ teaspoon salt

2 teaspoons cornstarch

1¼ cups freshly squeezed lemon juice (about 5 lemons), divided

1 cup fresh or frozen (thawed and drained) blackberries

7 large eggs

Powdered sugar, for sprinkling

Preheat the oven to 350 degrees F and lightly grease a 9 x 13-inch baking pan.

In a large bowl, combine the butter, ½ cup of the sugar, and 1 teaspoon of the lemon zest; beat with an electric mixer on medium speed until light and fluffy, about 2 minutes.

In a medium bowl, whisk together 2 cups of the flour and the salt until combined. Add the flour mixture to the butter mixture and stir by hand just until combined. Press the dough evenly into the bottom of the prepared baking pan; refrigerate for 15 minutes. Remove from refrigerator and bake until lightly browned, 15 to 20 minutes. Cool in the pan on a wire rack.

To make the sauce, combine 2 tablespoons of the granulated sugar, cornstarch, and ¼ cup of the lemon juice in a small saucepan; whisk to blend. Add the blackberries and cook over medium heat, stirring constantly and pressing on berries with the back of the spoon to extract juice, until mixture simmers and slightly thickens, 6 to 7 minutes. Strain mixture through a wire mesh strainer into a clean bowl, pressing on solids. Discard solids and reserve sauce.

To make the filling, whisk together the eggs, the remaining 3 cups granulated sugar, the remaining 2 tablespoons lemon zest, and remaining 1 cup flour until combined. Gradually add the remaining 1 cup lemon juice and whisk until combined. Pour mixture evenly over cooled crust. Spoon dollops of the blackberry sauce over the surface of the lemon filling. Drag a toothpick through the sauce to create swirls.

Carefully place the pan in the oven and bake until filling is set and edges are lightly browned, 30 to 35 minutes. Remove from oven and cool on a wire rack to room temperature. Cut into bars and sprinkle with powdered sugar.

Cranberry Oatmeal Cookies

These chunky oatmeal cookies with tart dried cranberries and sweet white chocolate chips offer deliciousness in every bite. For soft, chewy cookies, bake just until the edges are barely browned.

MAKES ABOUT 4 DOZEN COOKIES

1½ cups all-purpose flour

1 teaspoon baking soda

¾ teaspoon salt

½ teaspoon ground cinnamon

1 cup unsalted butter, softened

¾ cup granulated sugar

¾ cup firmly packed dark brown sugar

2 large eggs

1 teaspoon vanilla extract

3 cups old-fashioned rolled oats

1 cup white chocolate morsels

1 cup dried cranberries

Preheat the oven to 350 degrees F and line a baking sheet with parchment paper.

In a medium bowl, whisk together the flour, baking soda, salt, and cinnamon; reserve.

In a large bowl, combine the butter, granulated sugar, brown sugar, eggs, and vanilla; beat until smooth. Add the flour mixture to the butter mixture and beat until smooth.

Stir in the oats by hand until well combined. Add the white chocolate and dried cranberries and stir until evenly incorporated. Drop dough by rounded tablespoons onto the prepared baking sheet, 2 to 3 inches apart. Use fingers to flatten slightly. Bake until edges are just lightly browned (do not overbake), 9 to 10 minutes. Remove from oven, cool on the pan for 1 minute, and then transfer to a wire rack to finish cooling. Repeat with the remaining dough.

Strawberry Shortcake Cookies

This recipe combines the flavors of the perennially popular dessert in a convenient cookie form. Fresh strawberries and heavy cream comingle in the rich, buttery batter, and a sprinkle of sparkling sugar gives the cookies a sweet, crunchy finish.

MAKES ABOUT 3 DOZEN COOKIES

2 cups finely chopped fresh strawberries

2 teaspoons freshly squeezed lemon juice

1/2 cup plus 2 tablespoons granulated sugar, divided

1/4 teaspoon fresh lemon zest

2 cups all-purpose flour

2 teaspoons baking powder

1/4 teaspoon salt

6 tablespoons cold unsalted butter, cut into small pieces

2/3 cup heavy cream

Sparkling sugar, for sprinkling

Preheat the oven to 375 degrees F and line 2 baking sheets with parchment paper.

In a small bowl, stir together the strawberries, lemon juice, and 2 tablespoons of the sugar. Let stand for 15 minutes, stirring occasionally to distribute juices.

In a large bowl, stir together the lemon zest and remaining 1/2 cup sugar. Add the flour, baking powder, and salt; whisk to combine. Cut in the butter until mixture resembles coarse crumbs.

Add the cream and stir just until dough starts to come together. Add the strawberry mixture including juices and fold gently just until incorporated; do not overmix.

Drop rounded tablespoons of dough about 2 inches apart on prepared baking sheets. Flatten slightly and sprinkle with sparkling sugar. Bake until cookies are lightly browned, 10 to 14 minutes. Cool on the pan for 1 minute before transferring cookies to a wire rack to cool to room temperature.

Raspberry Streusel Crunch Bars

Toasted almonds add crunch and texture to the oatmeal cookie base of these super streusel bars. The doubly delicious filling contains both raspberry jam and raspberries.

MAKES 24 BARS

2$\frac{1}{2}$ cups all-purpose flour

$\frac{2}{3}$ cup granulated sugar

$\frac{1}{2}$ teaspoon salt

1$\frac{1}{4}$ cups unsalted butter, divided

$\frac{1}{2}$ cup old-fashioned oats

$\frac{1}{2}$ cup slivered almonds, toasted and chopped

$\frac{1}{4}$ cup firmly packed dark brown sugar

$\frac{3}{4}$ cup raspberry jam

$\frac{3}{4}$ cup fresh or frozen (thawed and drained) raspberries

1 tablespoon freshly squeezed lemon juice

Preheat the oven to 375 degrees F. Line a 9 x 13-inch baking pan with aluminum foil, leaving a 2-inch overhang on long sides; lightly grease the foil.

Whisk the flour, granulated sugar, and salt together in a large bowl. Cut 1 cup and 2 tablespoons of the butter into small pieces. Add butter to the flour mixture and beat with an electric mixer on low speed until the mixture resembles wet sand. Transfer 1$\frac{1}{4}$ cups of the mixture to a small bowl and reserve.

Press the remaining mixture into the prepared baking pan, making an even layer. Bake until the edges are lightly browned, 15 to 18 minutes.

To make the topping, add the oats, almonds, and brown sugar to the reserved flour mixture. Cut in the remaining 2 tablespoons butter until mixture forms pea-sized pieces; reserve.

In a small bowl, combine the jam, berries, and lemon juice; stir to blend. Remove the pan from the oven, cool for 1 minute, and spread evenly with the berry mixture. Sprinkle with the streusel topping, return the pan to the oven, and bake until filling bubbles and crust is browned, 22 to 25 minutes. Remove from oven and cool in pan on a wire rack for 1 hour. Remove from pan and cut into bars.

Blueberry Sugar Cookies with Lemon Cream Cheese Frosting

Forget chilling, rolling, or cutting; these sugar cookies loaded with juicy blueberries bake up fast and easy. Lemon zest and sour cream add tangy contrast to the sweet berries, and creamy frosting locks in moisture, keeping the cookies super soft.

MAKES ABOUT 3 DOZEN COOKIES

2½ cups all-purpose flour

1 teaspoon baking powder

¼ teaspoon salt

Zest of 2 lemons, divided

1 cup plus 2 tablespoons unsalted butter, softened, divided

1¼ cups granulated sugar

¼ cup sour cream

2 large eggs

Juice of 2 lemons, divided

1 cup fresh or frozen (thawed and drained) blueberries

8 ounces cream cheese, softened

4 cups powdered sugar

Preheat the oven to 350 degrees F and line 2 baking sheets with parchment paper.

In a medium bowl, whisk together the flour, baking powder, salt, and half of the lemon zest; reserve. In a large bowl, combine ½ cup plus 2 tablespoons of the butter with the granulated sugar; beat with an electric mixer on high speed until light and fluffy. Add the sour cream, eggs, and half the lemon juice; beat until incorporated. Slowly add the flour mixture and continue beating until combined. Gently fold in the blueberries.

Drop dough by rounded tablespoons on the prepared baking sheets, 2 inches apart. Bake until lightly brown around the edges, 12 to 14 minutes. Cool the cookies on the sheet for 1 minute then transfer to a wire rack to continue cooling to room temperature.

Combine remaining ½ cup butter and cream cheese in a medium bowl; beat with an electric mixer on high speed until smooth and creamy. Add remaining lemon zest and juice and beat until combined. Slowly add the powdered sugar, beating until smooth and creamy. Frost the cookies.

Pies
&
Tarts

Strawberry-Rhubarb Pie

Rhubarb pie or strawberry pie? Why pick just one? Tart rhubarb and sweet strawberries happily coexist in this deliciously old-fashioned pie that will remind you of Sunday dessert at Grandma's house.

MAKES 1 (9-INCH) PIE

2 unbaked (9-inch) pie pastries

1/3 cup water

2 tablespoons cornstarch

1 pound fresh rhubarb, chopped

1 cup plus 2 tablespoons granulated sugar

2 pints fresh strawberries, roughly chopped

2 tablespoons unsalted butter

1 egg yolk, lightly beaten

Vanilla ice cream or whipped cream, for serving

Preheat the oven to 400 degrees F. On a lightly floured work surface, roll out 1 pie pastry to a 12-inch round. Transfer to a 9-inch glass pie dish. Fold edge under, crimp, and reserve.

In a small dish, whisk together the water and cornstarch. In a large saucepan over medium heat, combine the rhubarb, 1 cup of the sugar, and the cornstarch mixture. Cook, stirring frequently, until thickened. Remove from heat and stir in the strawberries. Cool the mixture, uncovered, to room temperature. Pour into the pie dish and dot with butter.

On a lightly floured surface, roll out the second pastry to a 12-inch round. Cut into 12 strips, each 1 inch wide. Arrange 6 strips across the pie. Form lattice by weaving remaining 6 strips horizontally over and under first strips. Gently press ends into crust edges, trimming excess if necessary. Brush the lattice crust with the egg yolk then sprinkle with the remaining 2 tablespoons sugar. Bake until lightly browned and bubbly, 35 to 40 minutes. Cool pie on a wire rack to room temperature before slicing. Serve with vanilla ice cream or whipped cream, if desired.

Blueberry-Nectarine Pie

The peach's smaller, unfuzzy cousin has a lightly spicy flavor that pairs beautifully with sweet blueberries in this colorful fruit pie. Topped with a lattice crust, the pie is finished with a crispy cinnamon-sugar topping.

MAKES 1 (9-INCH) PIE

1 cup plus 1 tablespoon granulated sugar, divided

1/3 cup all-purpose flour

3/4 teaspoon ground cinnamon, divided

3 cups peeled, sliced fresh nectarines

1 cup fresh or frozen (thawed and drained) blueberries

2 unbaked (9-inch) pie pastries

1 tablespoon unsalted butter

1 tablespoon whole milk

Preheat the oven to 400 degrees F.

In a large bowl, whisk together 1 cup of the sugar, flour, and 1/2 teaspoon of the cinnamon. Add the nectarines and blueberries; toss to coat.

On a lightly floured work surface, roll 1 pie pastry to an 11-inch round. Fit the pastry to a 9-inch pie pan, trim to 1/2 inch beyond rim of pan, and crimp the edge. Fill pastry with the blueberry mixture and dot with butter.

Roll out the second pie pastry to a 12-inch round. Cut into 12 strips, each 1 inch wide. Arrange 6 strips across the pie. Form lattice by weaving remaining 6 strips horizontally over and under first strips. Gently press ends into crust edges, trimming excess if necessary.

In a small dish, whisk together the remaining 1 tablespoon sugar and remaining 1/4 teaspoon ground cinnamon. Brush the top crust with milk and sprinkle with the cinnamon-sugar mixture. Bake until crust is golden brown and filling is bubbly, 40 to 45 minutes. Cool on a wire rack.

Golden and Red Raspberry Tart

Golden raspberries have a sweet, mild flavor and a yellow-orange color. They are highly perishable, so if you cannot find them at the market, you can prepare this creamy tart with all red raspberries.

MAKES 1 (9-INCH) TART

1 unbaked (9-inch) pie pastry

8 ounces cream cheese, softened

1/2 cup granulated sugar, divided

1 teaspoon vanilla extract

2 teaspoons freshly squeezed lemon juice

2 cups heavy whipping cream, chilled

2 1/2 cups fresh golden or red raspberries, or a mixture of both

Preheat the oven to 425 degrees F. Fit the pie pastry into a 9-inch tart pan. Prick the bottom of the pastry with a fork. Line the pastry with foil and fill it with dried beans or pie weights. Bake until lightly browned, 20 to 25 minutes. Cool on a wire rack to room temperature.

In a large bowl, beat together the cream cheese, 1/4 cup of the sugar, vanilla, and lemon juice with an electric mixer until smooth.

In another large bowl, beat the cream with an electric mixer on high speed until foamy. Gradually add the remaining 1/4 cup sugar, beating on high speed until soft peaks form. Gently fold the whipped cream into the cream cheese mixture. Cover and refrigerate for 30 minutes.

Spoon the filling into the tart shell and smooth the top. Arrange the raspberries on top and refrigerate for 30 minutes before serving.

Variation: For a firm filling that will hold up at potlucks and parties, eliminate the lemon juice and substitute 1/2 teaspoon lemon zest in the cream cheese filling. Pour 1 tablespoon cold water in a small microwave-safe cup and sprinkle 2 teaspoons unflavored gelatin on top. Microwave on high for 10 to 15 seconds and stir to dissolve gelatin. Cool to room temperature. Just after beating the sugar into the whipped cream, add the cooled gelatin mixture and continue beating until stiff peaks form. Proceed with the rest of the recipe. Cover and refrigerate the tart for 2 hours before serving.

Strawberry Margarita Pie

The flavors of an icy Mexican cantina cocktail star in a sweet-tart pie that pairs fresh strawberries with a splash of lime juice and a kick of tequila (which can be substituted with orange juice). The pie can be made ahead and frozen for a perfectly cool dessert to serve after a spicy fiesta.

MAKES 1 (9-INCH) PIE

1¼ cups graham cracker crumbs

2 tablespoons granulated sugar

6 tablespoons unsalted butter, melted

3 cups halved fresh strawberries

1 (14-ounce) can sweetened condensed milk

¼ cup freshly squeezed lime juice (about 3 limes)

2 tablespoons tequila or orange juice

2 tablespoons orange juice

1 tablespoon fresh lime zest

1½ cups heavy whipping cream, chilled

Fresh whole strawberries, for garnish

Fresh lime slices, for garnish

Preheat the oven to 350 degrees F.

In a small bowl, whisk together the graham cracker crumbs, sugar, and butter. Press the mixture into the bottom and sides of a 9-inch pie pan. Bake the crust for 10 minutes. Cool on a wire rack to room temperature.

In a blender or food processor, combine the halved strawberries, condensed milk, lime juice, tequila, orange juice, and lime zest; process until completely smooth.

In a large bowl, beat the cream with an electric mixer on high speed until stiff peaks form.

Pour the strawberry mixture into a large bowl. Gently fold in the whipped cream. Spread the mixture in the crust and freeze until solid, 4 to 5 hours. Remove the pie from the freezer 1 hour before serving. Garnish with strawberries and lime slices and cut into wedges.

Cranberry-Apple Crunch Pie

Tangy cranberries and thinly sliced apples bake under a blanket of streusel in this blue ribbon pie packed with fall flavors. Dashes of nutmeg, cinnamon, and grated orange peel will fill your kitchen with a heavenly aroma.

MAKES 1 (9-INCH) PIE

1 unbaked (9-inch) pie pastry

3 large baking apples (such as Cortland or Jonathan), peeled and thinly sliced

1 tablespoon freshly squeezed lemon juice

2 cups fresh cranberries

1 cup firmly packed dark brown sugar, divided

1/4 cup cornstarch

1 tablespoon grated orange peel

1 teaspoon ground cinnamon

1/4 teaspoon ground nutmeg

5 tablespoons unsalted butter, divided

1/2 cup all-purpose flour

1/8 teaspoon salt

Preheat the oven to 350 degrees F. Fit the pie pastry inside a 9-inch pie pan.

In a large bowl, toss the apples with lemon juice; add the cranberries and stir. In a small bowl, combine 3/4 cup of the brown sugar, cornstarch, orange peel, cinnamon, and nutmeg; stir to combine. Add the brown sugar mixture to the apple mixture and toss gently to coat.

Crimp the edges of the pie pastry, fill with the apple mixture, and dot with 2 tablespoons of the butter.

In a small bowl, combine the flour, remaining 1/4 cup brown sugar, and salt; cut in remaining 3 tablespoons butter until crumbly. Sprinkle mixture over pie filling. Bake until filling is bubbly and topping is golden brown, 50 to 60 minutes. If necessary, cover edges with foil during the last 15 minutes to prevent overbrowning.

Boysenberry Galette

A free-form galette offers all the flavor of a crimped-crust pie with half the work. Boysenberries and pastry are baked to perfection in this unfussy French tart.

MAKES 1 (9-INCH) GALETTE

3 tablespoons granulated sugar

2 teaspoons cornstarch

2 cups fresh or frozen (thawed and drained) boysenberries or blackberries

1 unbaked (9-inch) pie pastry

1 large egg, beaten

Raw or sparkling sugar, for sprinkling

1 cup heavy whipping cream, chilled

2 tablespoons powdered sugar

1 teaspoon vanilla extract

Preheat the oven to 350 degrees F. Cut a piece of parchment paper to fit a baking sheet. Put the parchment paper on a work surface.

In a large bowl, whisk together the granulated sugar and cornstarch. Add the boysenberries and stir gently until coated with the mixture. Roll the pie pastry out to a 10-inch circle on the parchment paper; transfer the paper and pastry to the baking sheet. Carefully pour the boysenberry mixture inside the pastry to within 1 inch of the edge. Pleat and fold 1 inch of the pastry edge over the boysenberries and brush edges with the egg. Sprinkle edges with the raw sugar. Bake in the oven until filling bubbles and pastry is golden brown, 40 to 45 minutes.

In a large bowl, combine the whipping cream and powdered sugar and beat with an electric mixer on high speed until soft peaks form. Add the vanilla and continue beating until stiff peaks form. Reserve in the refrigerator until ready to serve.

Remove the galette from the oven and cool on a wire rack for 5 to 10 minutes before slicing. Serve warm topped with whipped cream.

Rustic Mixed Berry Tart

The unstructured shape of this cream-filled mixed berry tart is part of its charm, and it is also simple to make. The flaky tart shell is made from frozen puff pastry, and the creamy filling gets a citrusy lift from prepared lemon curd.

SERVES 6 TO 8

1 sheet frozen puff pastry (from a 17.3-ounce box), thawed in refrigerator

2/3 cup plus 2 teaspoons granulated sugar, divided

1 large egg

1/4 cup seedless raspberry jam

8 ounces cream cheese, softened

1/4 cup heavy cream

2/3 cup prepared lemon curd*

2/3 cup fresh blackberries or boysenberries

2/3 cup fresh raspberries

2/3 cup fresh blueberries

Powdered sugar, for dusting

Preheat the oven to 425 degrees F and line a baking sheet with parchment paper.

On a lightly floured work surface, unfold the thawed puff pastry and gently roll into a 10 x 11-inch rectangle. Transfer to the prepared baking sheet. Brush edges with water and fold edges over about 3/4 inch on all four sides to create a lip. Poke holes in the center of the pastry with a fork to facilitate crisp baking. Gently brush the entire tart with the egg and sprinkle with 2 teaspoons of the granulated sugar. Bake until golden brown, 15 to 20 minutes. Remove from oven, transfer to a wire rack, and cool to room temperature.

In a small saucepan, cook the jam over medium heat, stirring frequently, until it melts and liquefies. Remove from heat and reserve.

In a small bowl, combine the cream cheese, cream, lemon curd, and remaining 2/3 cup sugar; stir until blended. Spread the mixture in the center of the tart shell. Scatter the blackberries, raspberries, and blueberries on top of the filling. Drizzle with the warm jam. Let sit at room temperature for 10 minutes. Dust with powdered sugar and serve.

Available in some grocery stores and specialty markets.

Strawberry-Banana Ice Cream Cone Pie

Crushed sugar ice cream cones form the crust for this multilayered ice cream pie, which can be prepared ahead of time and frozen. Just thaw and serve for an easy anytime dessert.

MAKES 1 (10-INCH) PIE

1 (5¼-ounce) package sugar ice cream cones, finely crushed

5 tablespoons salted butter, melted

2 cups vanilla ice cream, softened

2 medium-sized ripe bananas, mashed

2 large firm bananas, cut into ¼-inch slices

2 cups strawberry ice cream, softened

1 pint fresh whole strawberries

1 cup heavy whipping cream, chilled

1 tablespoon powdered sugar

1 teaspoon vanilla extract

Grease a 10-inch pie dish. In a large bowl, combine the crushed ice cream cones and butter. Press the mixture into the bottom and sides of the pie dish. Cover and refrigerate for 30 minutes.

In a large bowl, combine the vanilla ice cream and mashed bananas. Spread the mixture over the crust; cover and freeze for 30 minutes. Arrange the sliced bananas over the ice cream; cover and return to freezer for 30 minutes. Top with strawberry ice cream; cover and return to freezer for 45 minutes.

Reserve 1 unhulled, unblemished strawberry for garnish. Hull the remaining strawberries, cut in half, and arrange around the edge of the pie.

In a large bowl, whip the cream and powdered sugar with an electric mixer on high speed until soft peaks form. Add the vanilla and continue beating for 1 minute. Mound the whipped cream in the center of the pie. Cover and freeze for at least 2 hours. Remove from the freezer about 30 minutes before serving and garnish center of pie with reserved strawberry.

Blackberry Custard Pie

Once a café staple, classic custard pie is making a culinary comeback. You will understand why when you taste this combination of rich, silky filling enveloping juicy blackberries in a golden crust.

MAKES 1 (9-INCH) PIE

2 cups fresh or frozen (thawed and drained) blackberries

1 baked (9-inch) pie crust, well chilled

1 tablespoon all-purpose flour

1 cup granulated sugar

1/8 teaspoon salt

1 cup evaporated milk

3 large eggs, lightly beaten

1 teaspoon vanilla extract

Preheat the oven to 425 degrees F.

Spread the blackberries evenly in the pie crust.

In a medium bowl, whisk together the flour, sugar, and salt. Gradually add the evaporated milk, stirring until smooth. Whisk in the eggs and vanilla until blended; pour mixture over blackberries. Bake for 15 minutes. Remove pie from oven and cover edges with aluminum foil to prevent overbrowning. Reduce oven temperature to 350 degrees F.

Return pie to oven and bake until filling is set, about 35 minutes longer. Cool on a wire rack to room temperature before slicing.

Country Blueberry Pie

This quintessential fruit pie has a woven lattice crust that is as practical as it is pretty. The gaps between the strips allow the steam from the juicy blueberry filling to escape during baking, which prevents the crust from getting soggy.

MAKES 1 (9-INCH) PIE

2 unbaked (9-inch) pie pastries

3/4 cup granulated sugar, plus extra for sprinkling

2 tablespoons plus 1 teaspoon cornstarch

1/2 teaspoon ground cinnamon

1/2 cup water

3 cups fresh or frozen (thawed and drained) blueberries

1 tablespoon freshly squeezed lemon juice

On a lightly floured work surface with a lightly floured rolling pin, roll 1 pie pastry from the center of the dough outward. Lift the dough, turn by a quarter, and repeat the rolling until the dough is 12 inches in diameter. Roll the dough gently onto the rolling pin and transfer it to a 9-inch pie pan. Unfold and ease the dough into the bottom of the pie pan without stretching it. Repeat the rolling process with the other disc of dough. Refrigerate dough while making filling.

Preheat the oven to 425 degrees F. In a medium saucepan, combine the sugar, cornstarch, cinnamon, and water over medium-high heat. Cook, stirring constantly, until mixture thickens, 4 to 5 minutes. Remove from heat and cool for 3 minutes. Add the blueberries and lemon juice and stir to blend.

Pour the filling into the dough-lined pie pan and top with the second pastry. Cut vents, flute the rim, and sprinkle the top lightly with sugar. Place pie on a baking sheet and bake for 20 minutes. Reduce heat to 350 degrees F and continue baking until top is lightly browned, 20 to 25 minutes. Cool pie on a wire rack for at least 20 minutes before cutting.

Desserts

CJ's Two-Berry Double Cream Parfaits

These Goldilocks-approved parfaits are not too tart and not too sweet. The balance of sweetened berries, tangy Greek yogurt, and vanilla bean ice cream is just right.

SERVES 6

1 3/4 cups fresh raspberries, divided

3/4 cup water

1/4 cup granulated sugar

2 tablespoons cornstarch

2 cups sliced fresh strawberries

2 teaspoons freshly squeezed lemon juice

1 pint best-quality vanilla bean ice cream

1 cup full-fat plain Greek yogurt

Combine 3/4 cup of the raspberries and the water in a medium saucepan. Heat over medium-high heat until mixture comes to a boil. Reduce heat to medium low and simmer for 20 minutes, skimming any foam that rises to the surface. Remove from heat and strain the mixture through a fine mesh strainer into another medium saucepan, pressing down on the solids to extract as much liquid as possible. Discard solids.

In a small bowl, whisk together the sugar and cornstarch. Whisk the sugar mixture into the strained fruit mixture. Heat over medium and cook, whisking frequently, until mixture thickens and starts to simmer. Cook for 2 more minutes then remove from heat and cool to room temperature. Add the remaining 1 cup raspberries, strawberries, and lemon juice; stir to combine. Transfer to a covered container and refrigerate for at least 2 hours.

In 6 chilled parfait glasses, layer the ice cream, berry sauce, Greek yogurt, and more berry sauce. Repeat layers.

Sweet Berry Tiramisu

This departure from the traditional Italian espresso dessert pairs a medley of strawberries, blueberries, and raspberries with a sweet, fluffy mascarpone cream. Ladyfingers are brushed with fruity framboise and spread with jam before the dessert is assembled into layered, luscious deliciousness.

SERVES 6 TO 8

1½ cups heavy cream

8 ounces mascarpone cheese, softened

1 cup granulated sugar, divided

1 teaspoon vanilla extract

5 tablespoons raspberry liqueur (such as framboise), or raspberry or blueberry syrup, divided

2/3 cup strawberry jam

1½ cups sliced fresh strawberries

1 cup fresh raspberries

½ cup fresh blueberries

20 ladyfingers

Spray a 9 x 9-inch baking dish with nonstick spray.

In a large bowl, beat the heavy cream until soft peaks form, 3 to 4 minutes. Beat in the mascarpone, ½ cup of the sugar, vanilla, and 2 tablespoons of the raspberry liqueur. Beat until smooth; reserve. In a small bowl, combine the jam and the remaining 3 tablespoons raspberry liqueur and stir until blended; reserve.

In a medium bowl, combine the strawberries, raspberries, and blueberries with the remaining ½ cup sugar, stirring well to coat berries. Cover and let sit at room temperature for 30 minutes, stirring occasionally; reserve.

Arrange half of the ladyfingers in the bottom of the pan, cutting to fit if necessary. Spread half of the cream mixture over the ladyfingers and smooth with a spatula. Spread with half of the jam mixture and use a knife to lightly swirl the jam into the cream layer. Top with half of the berry mixture. Repeat the layers. Cover and refrigerate until cream mixture is set, about 4 hours. Cut into squares and serve cold.

Blackberry Cobbler

The best things in life are often the simplest, which is definitely the case with this sweet blackberry cobbler. Topped with a tender, biscuity dough and baked to golden perfection, this cobbler needs only the adornment of vanilla ice cream.

SERVES 6

2$\frac{1}{2}$ cups fresh or frozen (thawed and drained) blackberries

1 cup granulated sugar

1 cup all-purpose flour

2 teaspoons baking powder

$\frac{1}{2}$ teaspoon salt

1 cup whole milk

$\frac{1}{2}$ cup unsalted butter, melted

$\frac{1}{2}$ teaspoon vanilla extract

Vanilla ice cream, for serving

Preheat the oven to 375 degrees F.

In a medium bowl, combine the blackberries and sugar. Let stand for 20 minutes, stirring occasionally.

In a large bowl, whisk together the flour, baking powder, and salt. Add the milk, butter, and vanilla; stir until blended. Spread the batter in an ungreased 8-inch square pan. Spoon the blackberry mixture over the batter.

Bake until the crust is brown and the filling is bubbling, 45 to 50 minutes. Serve warm topped with ice cream.

Strawberry Chocolate Chip Shortcakes

Is it possible to improve a trusted classic like strawberry shortcake? This fresh preparation just might find a permanent place in your recipe box. Sweetened berries, biscuits studded with chocolate, and sweetened whipped cream combine for an unforgettable combination.

SERVES 8

---

2 pounds fresh strawberries, sliced

1 cup granulated sugar, divided

2 cups all-purpose flour

2 teaspoons baking powder

1/8 teaspoon salt

1/2 cup unsalted butter, chilled, cut into 1/2-inch cubes

1 cup milk

1/3 cup mini chocolate chips, plus extra for garnish

1 1/2 cups heavy whipping cream, chilled

2 tablespoons powdered sugar

Preheat the oven to 400 degrees F and line a baking sheet with parchment paper.

In a large bowl, combine the strawberries and 3/4 cup of the granulated sugar and stir to coat. Let stand for 20 minutes, stirring occasionally.

Meanwhile, combine the flour, remaining 1/4 cup sugar, baking powder, and salt in a food processor; process to mix. Add the butter and process just until the mixture resembles coarse meal. Add the milk and pulse just until combined. Fold in the chocolate chips by hand; do not overmix.

Transfer the dough to a lightly floured work surface and divide into 8 portions. Use hands to roll portions into balls. Arrange dough balls 2 inches apart on prepared baking sheet. Use the heel of your hand to slightly flatten the balls to about 3/4 inch thick. Bake shortcakes until tops are golden brown, about 15 minutes. Remove from oven and cool on pan for 1 minute before transferring to a wire rack to finish cooling to room temperature.

In a large bowl, combine the cream with the powdered sugar and beat with an electric mixer on high speed until stiff peaks form.

Use a serrated knife to split each shortcake in half. To serve, place the bottom half of a shortcake on a dessert plate; top with some of the strawberries and some of the whipped cream.

Replace the top of the shortcake and top with additional whipped cream and berries. Sprinkle with additional chocolate chips.

Blueberry-Lemon Sherbet

With just five ingredients, this easy homemade sherbet is extra smooth because it is churned in an automatic ice cream maker. Buttermilk and lemon zest bring out the flavors of sweet puréed blueberries, making a pretty lavender-hued treat.

MAKES ABOUT 4 ½ CUPS

3 cups fresh or frozen (thawed and drained) blueberries

1 cup granulated sugar

1 cup buttermilk

Finely grated zest of 1 lemon

¼ teaspoon lemon extract

Combine the blueberries and sugar in a food processor or blender and process until smooth. Pour through a fine mesh strainer set over a bowl, pressing down on the solids to extract as much liquid as possible. Discard solids. Transfer mixture to a large bowl and add the buttermilk, lemon zest, and lemon extract. Stir until well blended.

Freeze the blueberry mixture in an ice cream maker according to the manufacturer's instructions. Transfer to a freezerproof container and freeze until firm, at least 2 hours. Sherbet will keep in the freezer, tightly covered, for up to 10 days.

Raspberry-Mango Sorbet

Give this sorbet a whirl in your ice cream maker when you are craving a tropical treat. A squeeze of fresh lime juice enlivens the bright, fruity flavors of sweet raspberries and ripe mangoes.

MAKES ABOUT 5 CUPS

3/4 cup granulated sugar

1 1/2 cups water

1 1/2 cups cubed mangoes

1 1/2 cups fresh or frozen (thawed and drained) raspberries

1/4 cup freshly squeezed lime juice (about 3 limes)

In a small saucepan, bring the sugar and water to a boil over medium-high heat. Cook and stir until sugar is dissolved. Remove from heat and cool to room temperature.

Place the mangoes and raspberries in a food processor; add sugar syrup and the lime juice. Cover and process until puréed. Pour the mixture into an ice cream maker and freeze according to manufacturer's instructions. Transfer to a freezerproof container and freeze until firm, at least 2 hours. Sorbet will keep in the freezer, tightly covered, for up to 10 days.

Mixed Berry Trifle

A straight-sided glass trifle dish will make the prettiest presentation for this show-stopping layered dessert, but you can also serve it in a large glass bowl. Sweetened condensed milk is the surprise ingredient that thickens and sweetens the creamy vanilla filling.

SERVES 8

2 cups heavy whipping cream, chilled

1 cup whole milk

1 (5.1-ounce) package vanilla instant pudding

1 (14-ounce) can sweetened condensed milk, chilled

1 pound fresh strawberries, sliced

1/2 pound fresh blackberries or boysenberries

1/2 pound fresh raspberries

1/4 cup cranberry-raspberry juice

1/2 cup granulated sugar

2 (12-ounce) angel food loaf cakes, cut into 1-inch cubes

In a large bowl, beat the cream with an electric mixer on high speed until stiff peaks form. In another large bowl, combine the milk and pudding mix and whisk until well blended. Add the sweetened condensed milk and whisk until smooth. Gently fold in the reserved whipped cream. Cover and refrigerate until ready to use.

In a large bowl, gently combine the strawberries, blackberries, raspberries, and cranberry-raspberry juice. Sprinkle with the sugar and gently stir to combine. Let sit at room temperature for 20 minutes, stirring occasionally to distribute juice and dissolve sugar.

Arrange one-third of the angel food cake cubes in the bottom of a 3-quart glass trifle dish or bowl. Spread with one-third of the cream mixture. Top with one-third of the berry mixture. Repeat the layers two times. Cover and refrigerate for 1 hour to set.

Strawberry Frozen Custard

Frozen custard is the richer, creamier cousin of regular strawberry ice cream. A base of half-and-half, egg yolks, and heavy cream plus a spin in the ice cream maker give the custard a silky-smooth texture that will melt in your mouth.

MAKES ABOUT 1$\frac{1}{2}$ QUARTS

1$\frac{1}{2}$ cups half-and-half

1 cup plus 1 tablespoon granulated sugar, divided

1 teaspoon vanilla extract

4 large egg yolks

1$\frac{1}{2}$ cups heavy whipping cream

$\frac{1}{2}$ pound fresh or frozen (thawed and drained) strawberries

Stir together the half-and-half, 1 cup of the sugar, and vanilla in a medium saucepan over medium-low heat. Heat the mixture just until bubbles start to form at the edge of the pan.

In a large bowl, whisk the egg yolks until they start to lighten in color, about 2 minutes. Slowly drizzle $\frac{1}{2}$ cup of the hot half-and-half mixture into the bowl with the eggs, whisking constantly.

Add the egg yolk mixture to the rest of the half-and-half mixture and cook over medium-low heat, stirring constantly, until mixture coats the back of a spoon. Strain through a fine mesh strainer into

a medium bowl. Add the cream and stir to combine. Cover and refrigerate for 2 hours.

Combine the strawberries and the remaining 1 tablespoon sugar in a blender or food processor and process until smooth. Remove the custard mixture from the refrigerator, add the strawberry purée, and stir to combine. Pour the mixture into an ice cream maker and freeze according to manufacturer's instructions. Transfer mixture to a freezerproof container, cover, and freeze until firm, about 2 hours.

Raspberry-Peach Granola Crisp

Ripe peaches and sweet raspberries pair up in this old-fashioned dessert with a modern twist. Use your favorite granola for the crunchy, buttery topping, and serve the crisp warm from the oven with vanilla ice cream.

SERVES 8

1½ pounds firm, ripe peaches (6–8 peaches)

2 teaspoons fresh lemon zest

2 tablespoons freshly squeezed lemon juice

½ cup granulated sugar

¼ cup all-purpose flour

2 cups fresh or frozen (thawed and drained) raspberries

2 cups prepared granola

4 tablespoons unsalted butter, softened

Vanilla ice cream, for serving

Preheat the oven to 350 degrees F. Grease a shallow 2-quart baking dish. Fill a large bowl with water and ice; set aside.

Fill a large saucepan two-thirds full of water and bring to a boil over medium-high heat. Use a slotted spoon to immerse the peaches, one at a time, in boiling water for 30 seconds to 1 minute, until their skins peel off easily. Place them immediately in ice water for 30 seconds. Drain and peel the peaches, slice them, and place them in a large bowl. Add the lemon zest, lemon juice, sugar, and flour. Toss well. Gently mix in the raspberries. Allow the mixture to sit for 5 minutes. Spoon into the prepared baking dish.

In a medium bowl, use hands to combine the granola with the butter until mixture resembles large peas; scatter over the peach-raspberry mixture. Bake until topping is lightly browned and fruit is bubbling, 20 to 30 minutes. Serve warm with vanilla ice cream.

Strawberry Panna Cotta

Panna cotta means "cooked cream" in Italian, and the lightly sweetened vanilla pudding is a perfect foundation for a homemade sauce of fresh strawberries. The secret to creamy, silky panna cotta is to cook the milk and cream mixture without letting it boil; allow the mixture to cool to room temperature before chilling.

SERVES 4

1½ cups whole milk

1 (¼-ounce) envelope unflavored gelatin

½ cup granulated sugar, divided

1½ cups heavy whipping cream

4 teaspoons vanilla extract, divided

1 quart fresh strawberries

¼ cup water

Pour the milk into a small bowl and sprinkle the gelatin on top. Let sit at room temperature for 5 to 10 minutes to soften gelatin.

Combine ¼ cup of the sugar and the cream in a saucepan over medium heat. Add the milk mixture and stir to combine. Cook, stirring often, until gelatin dissolves completely, about 3 minutes. (Do not allow mixture to boil.) Add 2 teaspoons of the vanilla. Pour the mixture into 4 (8-ounce) ramekins. Cool to room temperature. Cover and refrigerate until set, about 4 hours.

Reserve 4 strawberries for garnish. Hull and quarter the remaining strawberries and transfer to a medium saucepan. Add the remaining ¼ cup sugar, the remaining 2 teaspoons vanilla, and the water; heat the berries over medium. Cook, crushing strawberries with a potato masher or metal spoon, until mixture comes to a simmer and sugar dissolves. Simmer the sauce, stirring often, until it thickens, about 10 minutes. Cool to room temperature. Cover and refrigerate for 2 hours.

Just before serving, remove the ramekins from the refrigerator and dip the bottoms of the cups in warm water to help loosen the custard. Run a thin-bladed knife around the inner edge of each ramekin, turn onto a dessert plate, tap gently, and remove to unmold. Spoon the strawberry sauce over the panna cotta and garnish with reserved strawberries, whole or sliced.

Pavlovas and Cream with Berries and Fruit

Light-as-air pavlovas may look difficult to make, but the slow-baked meringue bases for this layered dessert could not be easier. After they have been spread with sweetened cream and topped with fresh fruit, the pavlovas should be eaten right away to preserve their crispy texture.

SERVES 10

5 large egg whites, at room temperature

Pinch of salt

1/4 teaspoon cream of tartar

1 cup granulated sugar

1 1/4 cups heavy whipping cream, chilled

2 tablespoons powdered sugar

1/2 teaspoon vanilla extract

1 1/2 cups fresh strawberries, roughly chopped

1 cup fresh raspberries

2 medium peaches, peeled and chopped

Preheat the oven to 225 degrees F and cut 2 pieces of parchment paper to fit 2 baking sheets. Trace a round 3-inch bowl with a pencil to make 5 circles on each piece of parchment paper. Flip the paper over and line the baking sheets.

In a large bowl, beat the egg whites with an electric mixer at medium speed until foamy. Add the salt and cream of tartar and beat on medium-high speed until soft peaks form. Add the sugar 1 tablespoon at a time and beat on high speed until stiff peaks form.

Use a spoon to divide the mixture among the 10 circles on the parchment paper, using the outlines as guides to make round shells with slightly indented centers. Bake until pavlovas are dry to the touch, 50 to 60 minutes. Turn off the oven and leave the pans inside for 2 hours to finish cooking. Remove the pavlovas from the parchment paper and transfer to a wire rack.

In a large bowl, combine the cream, powdered sugar, and vanilla; beat with an electric mixer on high speed until soft peaks form.

In a medium bowl, combine the strawberries, raspberries, and peaches. Spoon the berry mixture in the center of the pavlovas and top with sweetened whipped cream. Serve immediately.

Index

Metric Conversion Chart

VOLUME MEASUREMENTS		WEIGHT MEASUREMENTS		TEMPERATURE CONVERSION	
US	Metric	US	Metric	Fahrenheit	Celsius
1 teaspoon	5 ml	1/2 ounce	15 g	250	120
1 tablespoon	15 ml	1 ounce	30 g	300	150
1/4 cup	60 ml	3 ounces	90 g	325	160
1/3 cup	75 ml	4 ounces	115 g	350	180
1/2 cup	125 ml	8 ounces	225 g	375	190
2/3 cup	150 ml	12 ounces	350 g	400	200
3/4 cup	175 ml	1 pound	450 g	425	220
1 cup	250 ml	2 1/4 pounds	1 kg	450	230